Along FOR THE Ride

Elizabeth "Betsy" Lamude
2018

Along for the Ride

THE Ride

Scenes Through a Moving Window

Elizabeth Samuels

ARCHWAY PUBLISHING

Copyright © 2018 Elizabeth "Betsy" Samuels.
Interior Graphics/Art Credit: Elizabeth Samuels

All rights reserved. No part of this book may be used or reproduced by any means, graphic, electronic, or mechanical, including photocopying, recording, taping or by any information storage retrieval system without the written permission of the author except in the case of brief quotations embodied in critical articles and reviews.

Archway Publishing books may be ordered through booksellers or by contacting:

Archway Publishing
1663 Liberty Drive
Bloomington, IN 47403
www.archwaypublishing.com
1 (888) 242-5904

Because of the dynamic nature of the Internet, any web addresses or links contained in this book may have changed since publication and may no longer be valid. The views expressed in this work are solely those of the author and do not necessarily reflect the views of the publisher, and the publisher hereby disclaims any responsibility for them.

Any people depicted in stock imagery provided by Getty Images are models, and such images are being used for illustrative purposes only. Certain stock imagery © Getty Images.

ISBN: 978-1-4808-6167-1 (sc)
ISBN: 978-1-4808-6166-4 (e)

Library of Congress Control Number: 2018904225

Print information available on the last page.

Archway Publishing rev. date: 05/22/2018

Contents

Dedication ix
A Day in the Life of a Christmas Tree Farmer xi

Part One: Friends & Relations

Chapter 1   Virginia Beach and Norfolk, Virginia, ca. 1900-1960 1
Chapter 2   Galilee-by-the-Sea 3
Chapter 3   Mom 6
Chapter 4   Fall and Winter 12
Chapter 5   Gangs of My Youth 14
Chapter 6   The Summer Gang 17
Chapter 7   The Deli Life for Me 23
Chapter 8   Riding with Uncle Jim 26
Chapter 9   Horse 29
Chapter 10 Jack (Bill, Red, Son) Hayes 31
Chapter 11 God Bless Our Team… 34
Chapter 12 Returning to the Saga of
            Horse, the Wheeled Wonder: 37
Chapter 13 Motoring thru the Gene Pool 41
Chapter 14 Side Trip: Crabbing 47
Chapter 15 The Fabled F-150 53
Chapter 16 The Fourth 56

Part Two: Housekeeping 101

Chapter 17 Adventures in Housekeeping 71
Chapter 18 Blowing Snow 73
Chapter 19 Mud Flap 77

Chapter 20	And So She Rode Her Damp Mop Off Into the Sunset…	78
Chapter 21	House Vac Heart Attack	83
Chapter 22	News from El Rancho de los Ratons	85
Chapter 23	Country Winter	90
Chapter 24	While on the Subject of Good Neighbors…	94
Chapter 25	Continuing the Subject of Good Neighbors…	101
Chapter 26	Along for the Ride…	105
Chapter 27	The Beetle	108
Chapter 28	About the same time the Beetle entered our lives…	114
Chapter 29	To Every Thing…	116
Chapter 30	Grand Kids	120

Part Three: Adventures with Other-Legged Folks

Chapter 31	The Hawk of Foxfire	125
Chapter 32	The Colonel	126
Chapter 33	Sarge and the Deck Snow	131
Chapter 34	A Love Song for Snappy	133
Chapter 35	Carson's Cat	145
Chapter 36	Autobiographical Notes	150
Chapter 37	Collusion: It's an Amazing Thing…	153
Chapter 38	Things That Go WHUMP in the Night	154
Chapter 39	Trauma	156
Chapter 40	Jack Beagle is Churched	158
Chapter 41	A Fable about Big Jugs	165
Chapter 42	The Moonlight Run of Jack Beagle	168
Chapter 43	Ramblin' Man	170
Chapter 44	Jack Beagle Invents a New Game	172
Chapter 45	Possum in the Road	174
Chapter 46	Whistlin' Jack	176
Chapter 47	Episcomouse and the Antependium	180
Chapter 48	Why I Love Buckingham	184

About the Author ... 187

Dedication

To Daughter Amy's challenge to think of what fills us with gratitude on Thanksgiving Day I replied...

I am most thankful this and every day to have been a part of the ephemera that is *Foxfire*... a dream bit of land at the edge of the earth, just before one drops into the James River, just where the Blue Ridge starts its rise.

In my lifetime Foxfire has both brought and kept love and friends and family (two-, four-, and no-footed) foremost in heart and mind. It has been a joy in the good times and a solace in those others; it has brought countless happy times to the families who are strangers to us except for that once a year when they share the experience and magic of this place... and it has been the home of tall tales, guitar pickin', evergreens and river rats, and cousins, cousins, cousins...

Even those who are no longer with us, somehow, here at Foxfire, *are*.
Yep. Thankful Every Day...
This book is dedicated to Foxfire and all who have loved it.

A Day in the Life of a Christmas Tree Farmer

A couple of weeks ago I had an email asking if I would consider selling a Christmas tree in February. The customer had to cancel a regularly scheduled event at Christmas, and wanted to cut a tree now, late rather than never.

Of course I had no problem. I sell them when the customer wants them; so we set up a time for pick up, which was last Sunday afternoon.

The customers arrived about 2 p.m., two polite, nice looking, twenty-ish young men. We introduced ourselves, shook hands, and they were setting off to find their tree when curiosity got the better of me.

"Please don't hesitate to say if you'd rather I didn't know, but what's the occasion?"

Glances at one another, grins, and then "We're going to ride it down the stairs…."

Our nearest "urb" is a university town with many gracious old fraternity houses, so after I digested this intriguing bit of information, I asked: "Can I assume that there's a rather large amount of beer that goes into this project?"

Big grins and glances at one another. "Definitely. A **LOT** of beer!"

So many questions I failed to ask… but I suspect one of the old elegant frat houses in our nearby University town might well have been the venue for this ride.

Anyhow, I was at physical therapy for a knee problem yesterday, where there is a fine dry-erase board on which someone had last week drawn Katie Perry riding the big cat at the Super Bowl. During the week, someone had added the Left Shark, and when I admired it, my great therapist Tom said, yep, but I think it's about time to erase that and put up something new.

I went on with my exercises and told him about my February customer, so while I did my leg lifts, he drew a fine stick figure masterpiece of a fellow sliding down the stairs on a Christmas tree—sort of extreme surfing.

Everybody who came in loved the picture and got a laugh from the story, and there was lots of speculation about the particulars of the ride. I mentioned to the therapist that if one of his customers came in and said "Hey, that's me—I was there—" we'd know it was not an uneventful run.

I love my business. If they come back next year I'll ask if they'd like us to spray a little WD40 on their tree for them.

Part One

Friends & Relations

Chapter One

Virginia Beach and Norfolk, Virginia, ca. 1900-1960

The eldest of the relatives I remember from childhood were the five children of Harvey Lee Bailey and Zenetta Clarinda Boynton. All the family called Zenetta, Nettie, or Biboo; and her red-haired husband, Gadaddy.

Biboo's family, the Boyntons, had come ashore in Boston about 1639, married there, moved to Burlington, Vermont, and apparently prospered, inching southward to Arlington, Virginia, just prior to the Civil War. One of her brothers fought for the North and one for the South, and we can only imagine the turmoil of the family in dealing with this fact. We knew of this and a great deal of the Boynton history because one of our Lake Placid cousins wished to join the DAR and had thoroughly researched our "four bears", and she was good enough to share the research with us.

Of Gadaddy's family we knew little except for two characters who made a lasting impression because of some notable eccentricities. One of these, Uncle Nat, was known for his grim expression, never having cracked a smile at anything except once:

Our Mom was about four or five years old and lovingly raising a baby chick when the family cat came by and quickly put an end to the chick. Mother just as quickly grabbed the cat's tail and swung him around in a couple of perfectly described circles, heard a noise behind her, and it was Uncle Nat, about to split his sides laughing…

The other oddly memorable Bailey from that generation was Aunt Emma (this one an Ant, not Aunt). Aunt Emma gained notoriety for walking around everywhere with a hot water bottle on a rope hanging down her back; and for being the world's most frustrated jigsaw puzzler. The family would be thoroughly engrossed in putting a puzzle together and Aunt Emma would wander by, pick up a piece, and without regard for whether it could possibly fit where she put it, shove it in anyway, mumble "Oh, Jesus!" at the ensuing jumble, and wander off again, leaving in her wake her nonplussed fellow puzzlers.

CHAPTER TWO

Galilee-by-the-Sea

The Choir at Galilee Church, Va. Beach, Va. Ca 1900

Galilee Church was on the beachfront at 18th Street in Virginia Beach when this photo was taken. Sometime mid-1900's a new Galilee was built further north and a couple of blocks inland. The old church was lovely

3

and holds many happy memories, but I am sure today's parishioners have not missed the old Sunrise Service with the sun rising out of the beautiful ocean to shine on an enormous week-old washed up dead whale, whose aroma wilted all the Easter lilies.

http://www.galileechurch.net/#/home/history

The choir at the time of the photo above appears to have been about 25% red-headed Baileys, among them my Grandmother, Rosamund Corinne, (Auntie Blue), [third row, 1st from left]; Great Aunts Ruth [2nd row, fourth from left] and Lorenna, [4th row, 2nd from right, half hidden,] (Tookie and Auntie); and great Uncles I. B. (Uncle Brother) [2nd row, 5 from left]; and James (Uncle Jim) [front row, baby].

A look at those red heads and angelic faces will go a long way toward explaining why even as President of the local Women's Christian Temperance Union, their Mother carried a little blackberry cordial at all times "for medicinal purposes". She was a rotund soul, just over four feet tall and round enough that young grandchild Pibbie once asked her please to put a board across her knees so she could have a lap to sit on. While en route to her WCTU meeting one evening she slipped and fell, breaking the bottle of "medicine" in her purse... she presided over the meeting with great dignity nonetheless, all the while reeking of alcohol.

The childhood home for these angelic choristers was on 16th Street and Arctic a few blocks off the ocean in Virginia Beach, in a cedar shingled house built by our great-grandfather, master carpenter Harvey L. Bailey (Gadaddy), whose building projects included some of the lovely old resort hotels as well as the first Boardwalk at the Beach, and of course, the home he built for his wife, Zenetta Clarinda (*nee Boynton*) and his five red-haired cherubs. As they grew, four of the "angels" stayed close to home at Virginia Beach. The eldest brother, I.B., found and married his lovely Kate, and they lived and raised their family in North Carolina, so were not as much a part of the everyday life of the Bailey clan.

The other four were close enough that at any given time, they could be found living with spouse and progeny in the house of one of the others, whether in Norfolk, Virginia Beach, or halfway, in Oceana at Uncle Jim's house. When I was growing up, my grandmother and grandfather, my mother and father, and their daughters (sisters Skits and myself, and tiny sister Tobe) lived with Auntie and her husband Will, their adopted son Jack (actually Ruth's son); Jack's two sisters most of the time; and their mother, Ruth, when she was not in New York City, where she was an administrator in a vocational school. In summer, the whole shebang, along with whatever brother or sister or offspring thereof was passing thru, moved to my grandparents place in Virginia Beach. It all seemed to work very well, probably due in no small part to the fact that tempers and petty sniping never got much traction…Uncle Jim and Ruth (Tookie) could be volatile, but they rotated in and out. The core four were solidly united in family, and the family circle expanded and contracted as needed.

My grandparents built their Virginia Beach home at 317 16th Street, and when I was young, we spent cold weather months in Norfolk at Auntie's house, but summers were in the house on 16th where my Mother grew up.

front porch with hollyhocks

Chapter Three

Mom

The house my grandfather built at 317 16th street in Virginia Beach was a wonderful brick structure with a big 5 or 6 step up front porch suitable for roller skating. My Grandmother grew beautiful flowers, and the hollyhocks came up above the brick railing and watched us skate… In return, we helped ourselves to the fancy ballerina blooms and little loaf seed pods; and often caught in our quart jars one of the bumble bees that mumbled peaceably from plant to plant. The same quart jars were also used to collect Japanese beetles at a whopping nickel for a morning's catch… and later in the day, when dusk-dark arrived they came in handy for keeping our lightning bugs so they could light us to sleep. Below the porch rail along with the hollyhocks, were handsome larkspurs, some lots taller than I was… below those, petunias… and roses and hydrangeas anchoring the corners of the house. Our Grandmother, whom we called Auntie Blue, swore that her flowers were so beautiful because of "the feet of little children running through the beds".

It was from this house that our always practical grandfather decided to send Mom off to college because " Every woman needs to be trained to make a living".

Mom with her Father, W. W. Sawyer, ca 1930

"Pibbie"

Mark Twain: "I came in with Halley's Comet in 1835. It is coming again next year, and I expect to go out with it." Twain died on April 21, 1910, one day after perihelion, when the comet emerged from the far side of the sun.

And so it was with Mom (Elizabeth Sawyer Falconer, nicknamed by the Family, for no known reason, "Pibbie"). She came in on the same Halley's comet appearance that Mark Twain used for his exit, in July 1910, and always forecast her own exit at age 75, when the comet would come again. Happily for all, she stayed longer than that, not leaving until 1989. Halley must have been off-schedule.

In a family full of blue-eyed "carrot tops" she stood out like a sore thumb with her dark hair and eyes, and she spoke often of how tired she became of wearing reds and pinks as a youngster… shades forbidden to redheads in those days. She was the eldest of the group of first cousins, and they all looked up to her.

Our grandparents were not wealthy, but they were very comfortably ensconced in the rising middle class. They had the means to shower their only child, Mom, with things like her own specially blended perfume; an exquisite gold filigree ring made especially for her; fine clothing, leather riding boots, and in her "flapper" years, among other lovely clothes, long lame palazzo pants, her outfit replete with long cigarette holder.

It's probably no surprise that a young woman whose female kin encouraged independent thinking, and whose parents loved indulging her, should have some objections to being summarily shipped off to some God-forsaken town in rural central Virginia to attend the Farmville State Teacher's College. After all, it was the late twenties, the school was *forever* away from Virginia Beach via long train ride, and even the still infant long-distance phone service was unreliably available. But this stubborn young lady had met her match.

Young Pibbie feigned all manner of dire illnesses, to be sent home to recover, and then was bounced right back to Farmville by her determined Dad. She faked tonsillitis and even appendicitis, was sent home and actually had the offending parts removed… Then her folks shipped her right back to Farmville. And no one knows how many times she stepped on her glasses, smashing them so she'd have to return home to have new ones made…

Despite all this, and herself, she continued her teaching courses and pursued her second major, in music, specifically piano. Until arthritis arrived many years later, she had such a lovely touch at the piano. As a child I loved nothing more than sitting under her baby grand with my imaginary frogs, Daggety and Jupiter, and listening to her play.

By the time Farmville was growing on her, she was ready to graduate and leave, teaching certificate in hand. (Later, on a rare vacation trip, she proudly gave us a tour of her alma mater, now become Longwood University.)

The home she returned to was roomy and welcoming, and the fact that it was located in Virginia Beach made it a natural gathering place for our assortment of aunts, uncles, and cousins

a: when any of them needed a temporary lodging or

b: for holiday gatherings. I believe the ancestry of our gathering for the Fourth of July reunion/block party we now celebrate is rooted in the gatherings at that old house.

During our last years at that lovely place, we began losing family at a truly alarming rate, one a year from our household from 1942 to 1948. Counted among the loss were our grandparents, who passed away; and our father, who found something to do he thought was more important; and an infant baby brother, twin to sister Tobe.

Summing up: In about 5 years' time, Pibbie had lost both parents; her spouse of twelve years, father of her three daughters; and a baby. Add in the death of a couple more family elders along with her loss of any visible means of support, and the phrase "depths of despair" takes on real immediacy.

But the stalwart group of First Cousins, children of the generation decimated in those dark years, along with the two remaining elders, closed ranks around us and surely kept us kids from being traumatized forever by the changes; and that closeness kept our Mom from giving in to abject despair.

After a childhood of love and indulgence, she was now faced with being the sole support for her three young daughters and her recently widowed aunt.

Fortunately for all of us, underneath her beautiful face, above those knockout gams, lying dormant for her first thirty years, was an iron will, resolved that her family would survive.

Pibbie took her teaching certificate and went to work.

Since we three sisters, Skits, Tobe and I are six years apart in age, each of us grew up with a slightly different version of Mom; but all three of us are incredibly proud that we belonged to this indomitable spirit.

For a while, to keep afloat, we rented our upstairs rooms to summer tourists and all us kids moved to the room we called the back porch. It was wonderful to me… our renters were invariably interesting and good to us… but it was only a temporary patch on our financial needs. As the winter holiday approached, Mom saw no relief, and she asked if we, her children, wanted to sell her baby grand piano to pay for Christmas.

We did.

I'm not one generally given to remorse, but this one haunts me… and not just me. When Sister Skits graduated nursing school and landed her first job, her first major purchase was a new piano for Mom.

When modern washing machines became available, our Grandfather had purchased for his family one of the new-fangled things with a window in front for watching your sudsy clothes go 'round and 'round. He was transfixed, and watched it for hours on end. It was new technology, so of course a number of laundry items, notably woolens, came out of the washer much smaller than they went in. The Christmas we sold Mom's baby grand piano, Santa left a tiny Schoenhut piano for us kids… when Cousin Jack arrived for the holiday, his reaction: "Look… Pib put the piano in the new washer!" Our tribe of wonderful and irreverent cousins wouldn't let despair win out.

Then the ceiling fell in. No, really. A rare wet, heavy snow got under the roof tiles and into the attic, and collapsed the plaster ceiling.

Repair estimates were such that Mom would have had to mortgage the house, and she carried with her the caution of the father who had urged her thru college, that it was *never* good business to borrow. So she put the house her father and grandfather had built up for sale, and we moved from that lovely place to a duplex apartment on 22nd street… four small rooms and a bath. The up side was a large yard in front and a pond in back; and the upstairs rental apartment would bring in some much needed shekels for our little family,

In addition to teaching fifth grade, and later, middle-school age youngsters, since teachers were only paid 10 months of the year and she had food to buy and bills to pay 12 months of the year, Mom worked summers at the local 5 & 10 Cent Store. In those days the pay was about thirty five cents an hour. Even allowing for inflation, this wasn't much, but it kept us going during the long summers, along with The Summer Loan, which came about every year about the time school was out (and the paycheck from teaching ended). To make ends not meet, but at least be in shouting distance of one another, Mom would take out a smallish loan to help us get to September, when her paychecks would start again.

I am sure that J. P. Morgan or Cornelius Vanderbilt never agonized over a financial maneuver more than Mom did. All of us knew when she was in agony over some bump in her life's road: her bed was in the middle of the house, where access to any room necessitated going right by her little cubby with the badly sprung daybed where she slept each night. Seeing her there with the sheet pulled completely over her head, it didn't take genius to know some real agonizing was going on… Eventually she would make the trip to the bank, where I'm certain there was no hesitation about making her the loan because she'd never failed to repay, and we'd be o.k. for the days ahead; but the cost to her in having to go ask was enormous.

Mom worked late on weekends and during Christmas vacation at the local dime store so there would be a little extra money for Christmas for her three good girls. When she got home on Christmas Eve, after 9:30 pm, when the last of the local Santas had picked up their layaways at the dime store and they could finally close, she was ready to relax and unwind a bit. All the Cousins would be there at our house, several hours ahead of her in the eggnog, bourbon-and-branch department, and they'd rush to help her catch up with them… and they tell of the year they woke Christmas morning to find that Mom, having done her duties as Mrs. Claus, had mellowed out sufficiently by the time she went to bed, that she had carefully hung up HER stockings, both of them… on a nail … on the wall…with the girdle still attached!

Chapter Four

Fall and Winter

When I was very young we spent winters in Auntie's house on the Elizabeth River in Norfolk.

It was a roomy, comfortable house. I don't remember the precise configuration of it because in my memories it was always so full of Cousin Jack's buddies, high school age and onward, milling around the house, listening to Artie Shaw and Benny Goodman, and talking of, participating in, and coming home from college, the draft, and WWll. At six years old, my strongest impression was of leaping over or crawling under the long legs of young men (and women) draped over the furniture like human throws...

Hanging from one of those long legs was an enormous purple stump where there had once been a big toe, which was left somewhere in Germany, where its teen- aged owner had been navigator on a bomber until flak from below swept the offending digit away. Boys being boys, the group hanging out at Auntie's ragged the poor guy endlessly about getting a purple heart on the strength of his missing big toe; and invariably introduced him as "Ed, The Nine-Toed Wonder".

I do remember that the house had a basement (coal cellar) where Auntie had allowed to be set up a target range for .22 rifles. I expect this was to be as certain as possible that our young'uns came safely back from said war... Today, Social Services would lock up the whole crew of adults and throw away the key for exposing the rest of us to rifle fire a mere couple of inches below us. Times change: people, even young-ish ones, were expected to have common sense and exercise it.

A word about the times:

These early years were Wartime Years, and everyone was affected... I was about six when the war ended, but my memories include such things as air raid sirens and blackout curtains, which we all had; of helping crush tin cans by stomping on them "to build battleships"; of the newsreels at the theater of planes dropping bombs (even today the sound of an aircraft engine nearby brings back childhood terror); the black painted plywood at the end of each street at Virginia Beach, so the Germans couldn't see our lights; and even my misty memory of playing on the beach while everyone gathered to watch a U-Boat burn; all these and more things that made up the Wartime world affected all of us deeply and permanently.

Chapter Five

Gangs of My Youth

Living in homes seasonally was a wonderful thing because I got to enjoy two separate and equally wonderful sets of childhood friends.

The Winter Gang

The first gang I remember was a tough bunch hanging out on the streets of our little neighborhood in the city of Norfolk. I was five or six years old, known for a certain mulishness and perhaps a little creativity. My very best bud was a little girl I called "Banjo". We were close to the same age and spent a lot of time together riding tricycles, drawing paper dolls and making mudpies, some of which we actually sampled. The senior member of our gang was a tall slim youngster with pretty, dark, curls, named Louise. Because the heavyweight champion of the world was a big favorite at my house, Louise's nickname became "Joe Louis". She was a quiet youngster, who always came with her little sister, about three years old, in tow. Little Sister was known inside our gang and out as "Baby".

Like most urban gangs we had a wannabe hanger on. His name was Otto, and he was an early learning experience in the meaning of the expression "You don't want to stand too close to that one".

For some reason Otto decided to mark our house as his own—perhaps

Mom paid more attention to him than anyone else would—and one of his favorite ways to get her to notice him was to stand on our front porch on a nice sunny day and piddle through our screen door. This brought on reprimands of course, and some serious discussion as to why nice young men didn't do that. Otto paid no heed. He was getting the attention he craved.

Our connections with the post office had brought to our home an old fashioned set of postal shears, which were like scissors on steroids, huge and heavy as lead, about 16 inches long.

One day when she was completely fed up with cleaning up after Otto, Mom, being her patient self*, waited behind the door for him to make his daily pit stop. When she heard his feet at the door she opened it wide with the postal shears at the ready...

That was the last time Otto mistook us for a restroom.

Otto and I were of an age, but my imagination never held a candle to his. His favorite target was little runny nosed "Baby", and he enjoyed putting her under the outside faucet, turning the water on full blast... and *running!*

I think the howl she set up one of those times must have gotten on Otto's last nerve.

He came to our door and of course Mom went to greet him. He announced in a booming raspy voice 'way too big for his six year-old frame "I have a friendly little note for you" and he passed a grubby multifolded piece of paper to her, and, as usual, ran. Mom opened it carefully and read in 6-year old pencil-scrawl

"Baby is a Bitch"...

Even today in the family when a last nerve has been trodden upon by some obnoxious soul, the offended party will confide in the nearest sympathetic ear "I have a friendly little note for you..."

*Mom's Patience

After I reached the age of ten there were no men in our house, just Mom, the three sisters, our great aunt, a female SPCA dog and assorted female cats, so Mom got to be the General Factotum of repair. Her specialties were carpentry and, best of all, electrical repair. I remember the many, many times when she'd strip wires, working with her tongue stuck out just a little, with the same absolute concentration she gave earlier to playing Chopin's Nocturne in E-flat in the evening. She'd put one connector to the other, apply the electrical tape, and then give one of her three girls the plug to put in the socket for a test. We never discussed this, but I prefer to think that she felt she would be better able to do CPR on us than we could on her. Thank God, I don't remember anything blowing up...

Anyhow... She loved birdwatching, and my husband built her a bird feeder from a coffee can attached to two boards, and nailed it to the house where she could fill it from the kitchen window and see the birds up close and personal. She loved it.

Mom's house was on a pond, and there were ducks and geese galore, so it wasn't long before the old Muscovy ducks found the bird feeder, and cleaned it out at every opportunity. Mom shooed them off time after time, to no avail.

Any of her three daughters could have told the ducks they were playing a losing game.

So... Mom cut an old lamp off its cord, and stripped about ten inches of insulation back. Next she used brads to nail the wires down each side of the feeding platform about, say, ohhh... the width of duck feet apart. Then with the same patience she used to cure Otto, she sat by the window holding the plug close to the socket underneath, and waited...

She was still grinning when I saw her: "Darlin' you should have seen that duck... his red head feathers stood up just like a Mohawk and he said "W-a-a-a-a-c-k"!

She was a happy lady; and the old Muscovy used the same arcane communication ducks use to spread the word that food's available to let his buddies know about the bird-feeder from Hell.

Chapter Six

The Summer Gang

Virginia Beach, summer, mid-twentieth century:

If there was ever a better place to be a kid, I don't know where. Sister Skits and I would put on our white pinafores and sandals on warm summer evenings and take a basket of gardenias from our yard to sell to the tourists on the Boardwalk, and later spend our earnings on the oceanfront at the wonderful Carousel or the Ferris wheel, or maybe the miniature train.

The Gang of Summer changed slightly from time to time, but the regular players were:

My very best bud Helen, who lived a block back of us on 17th street, the main road into town at the time. There was a Texaco station next to her house so we could keep our bikes "aired up" at all times en route from one house to the other.

Jerry was my next door neighbor, and with Helen and I, the third member of the summer gang. She was tall, pretty, and really good at jumping rope.

…but to have a proper gang in town, same as a game of bridge, you need a Fourth. It takes four to be able to jump Double Dutch, two to turn, two to jump.

Four was a "snowbird" who spent winters in Norfolk, (19 miles away, but light years in urbanization) but moved to a cottage a couple of doors down in summer. Her name was Glenda. I was with her when

I was of the age to think that if I believed hard enough I could fly, and I launched myself off her ten-foot tall shed roof.

Guess what?! Shaken faith and a split lip, a step up from the chronically skinned knees I sported so often that my mother would paint big mercurochrome flowers on my knees to make them more attractive…

City-wise Glenda and her family introduced me to the urban phenomenon of the drive-in, where the waitresses wore roller skates, and you could try exotic things, like cheeseburgers or the new French-fried onion rings.

That foursome was the framework of the Summer Gang, often added to or subtracted from as families came and went. It was a group rich in heritage: one Roman Catholic who attended parochial school; one Jewish youngster, whose family was still coming to grips with the news coming back from Europe; one Methodist and one Episcopalian. We rode bikes on the smooth cement of 16th street til we nearly wore ruts. We chased the iceman's truck until he'd ice-pick off a sliver from his big ice block and hand it to us. We walked for miles with nothing but a foil bag of ice for sustenance, sometimes walking the circle where the Catholic church was located… often we'd meet the good Father P. P. Brennan, looking the picture of the sainted Irish clergyman. Though he was deaf as a post he invariably had a kind word and a dime for each of us (a change from my Uncle Jim. Father P. P. always crossed himself when he met Uncle Jim).

My family lived three blocks back from the ocean in summers in the lovely brick home my grandfather had built. My great-grandfather, a "master carpenter" who had been instrumental in building the first boardwalk at the Beach, was working on the original Princess Anne Hotel at the time our house was built, and put some of the "overage" in our house, including a lovely stained glass window at the stair landing. The landing was large enough for building blanket tents or for doll tea parties, and a nice rest between flights if you were bumping on your bottom on the waxed hardwood all the way downstairs.

On the second floor once a year my grandmother would pull all the mattresses off the beds and move them into the hall which ran the length of the house, and encourage us to bounce from one end to the other of this wonderful tumbling run. We may have been helping to get the old winter mustiness out, but I think it was more that she was the sort of grandmother who told people her flower beds were beautiful because of all the children's feet running thru them; and she appreciated what a fine day's fun it would be to bounce down that hall.

The rise-to-run on the beautiful hall staircase was such that as a preteen (only a preteen would do it) I liked to lie upside down on the stair rail when it was too hot to be outdoors, and read my current Nancy Drew or Hardy Boys books. There was always a cool breeze in the hall.

I linger a bit on that hall because it was the site of major "gang" activity in the summer season.

It seemed an unlikely spot at first glance, but if you looked at it from a theatrical point of view, it had fine places to enter from the kitchen (stage right), or pop out of the under-stair closet; or you could sweep theatrically down the stairs and be between the two fancy wood columns (we elegantly labeled these "first base" and "second base") at the living room entrance, where there was ample seating for a good sized audience. And what do you know… we took in summer boarders, and nearly always had a family or two vacationing in our upstairs winter bedrooms… and if they happened to notice our pre-production flyers, or chanced to come downstairs into the hall at the right moment in early evening there was no way they could escape our latest production.

Our version of Summer Theater rose from combined auspicious circumstances:

1. We had the Hall, a natural theatre; and a captive audience of boarders and family.

2. Helen had a wonderful front porch for roller skating, the best thing that happens to town kids (replaced now, I think, by skateboarding). We skated for hours on end, singing at the top of our lungs. Helen's family was kind to put up with it, interrupting only when her Dad, a big Wagner fan, would put on the RCA Red Labels, turn the Victrola all the way up, and listen to The Ring Cycle hours and days on end. You haven't really skated till you've skated to The Ride of the Valkyries… We became

thoroughly saturated with the Teutonic side of opera, Lohengrinned and Fausted, too. We hummed Wagner!

3. At home, Mom was more likely to put on Verdi or Bizet, and early on she put a couple of elaborately illustrated books about grand opera in my hands, and I was fascinated. The stories were wonderful, as were the breathtaking arias. Actually listening to a whole opera, not so much; I had a lot of outdoor time to get in. Still do when it comes to taking in a whole opera.*

4. …and the tipping point… Auntie (or my Grandmother) and Skits had taught me very early on how to sew, beginning with doll clothes, winding up with my wedding dress and clothes for my own little ones, but in between making all sorts of wonderful costumes, Hallowe'en and otherwise, of different colored crepe paper, 10 cents a big roll at the five-and-ten.

And so, you see, the stage was set. We became a Summer Theater Troupe!

Our gang's (ages 3 to about 10) productions were really more in the order of tableaux vivants, since our primary interest was in putting only the most notable arias on the Victrola and parading only the splashiest costumes… Our first production was Carmen, of course. Jerry, tall with curly hair, made a gorgeous Carmen with a flamenco outfit of black, red and pink crepe paper ruffles to die for. I remember trying to figure out how to do dark hair along with the lipstick and eye shadow, but settled for a fancy comb and a black mantilla someone had given Auntie. We had a toreador, sword, cape, and all, our Escamillo; and of course, Don Juan. Carmen the Temptress held forth with her rose between her teeth, right up to her tragic demise.

It was a smashing success! Enough applause to commit us to another performance, and enough dimes from family and boarders to buy crepe paper to make the next production's costumes… what more could an aspiring troupe want?

Neither Mom nor Helen's folks were fans of Gilbert and Sullivan, who would have been a gold mine of prospective theatre for us; but we took a stab at The Barber of Seville, Madame Butterfly and Pagliacci, stories of great loves mostly unrequited and ultimately gory with great opportunities for using knives and swords and lots of crepe paper ruffling in the costumes. We were all about swash, buckle and ruffle…

Our greatest success from a producer's point of view had to have been Wagner's "Lohengrin".

Casting was the first problem, overcome with the introduction of young blood into our troupe. The title role went to little Sister Tobe, just old enough to act (about 4 years old), yet young enough to be malleable**. With her short dark hair she was a logical choice for the male lead. She was no crepe-paper knight, but heavily aluminum-foiled in her gleaming princely armor, with a foil covered sword and a helmet made of a foil covered lampshade. Turned upside down, it was also a crown for the King. Fortunately, the King and Lohengrin were not in many scenes together in our version.

Elsa was played by the only gang member shorter than Tobe, a tiny blue-eyed blond three year old neighbor. Not much on lines, but looking every inch her part… she was a lovely, delicate crepe paper princess.

There was a full house opening night.

I don't remember whether we ever made it to the famed Bridal Chorus scene or not, because when Tobe entered stage right in all her gleaming aluminum glory, holding her sword in one hand and her lampshade helmet in place with the other, dragged by invisible extras in a Swan Boat that looked suspiciously like a galvanized wash tub with a homemade swan head attached, she brought down the house.

We made enough that night to buy crepe paper *and* aluminum foil!

*In the matter of the classics: Mom, who had trained as a classical pianist, would play for us all after supper every night. Auntie said it was to get out of washing dishes, but I could have listened to Mom play Chopin forever. He was and is yet my favorite, and her touch was perfect for his music.

**About four, young and malleable, was also when we decided Little Sister Tobe could be our Fourth for Bridge. There was Mom, and Auntie, Sister Skits and Yrs. Truly, but we were frequently one short, so Tobe was elected to sit hours as our Fourth when she would no doubt have much preferred doing something, anything, else. She turned into a fine bridge player. Wisdom came with age, though, and past the age of perhaps nine, malleable is not a word I'd ever have used in any description of Tobe. Thank goodness she continued to honor the commitment to bridge foisted upon her at such a tender age…

Lohengrin's Swan Boat in its other life:
the Author and Big Sister, Skits

Chapter Seven

The Deli Life for Me

I grew up two blocks from a little slice of heaven on 16th Street in Virginia Beach named Harry's Delicatessen.

The regular grocery stores in those days didn't carry the 10,000 items of today's supermarket, so if you wanted some really good Swiss cheese or pastrami or corned beef, Havarti or muenster, provolone or hard salami, (the names alone sound like music, don't they?) and the requisite loaf of fresh thin-sliced "pump" or rye bread and kosher dills to go with all this, Harry's Deli was the place to go.

Next door to Harry's at that time was The Fish Market. You could see the fishing boats on the ocean from the entrance to the store, and you could pick your dinner from the catch displayed on ice in the cases. Faster than the eye could follow your selection would be wrapped in newspaper and stuffed in a paper bag for the trip home.

A choice from either of these two side-by-side Gardens of Fragrant Delight would satisfy even the most discerning palate.

…but back to Harry's: Those wonderful cold cut sandwiches, always served with home-made potato salad (with celery and onion, no wussy sweet relish), were a ticket to gustatory heaven. When all the family piled into our little house we planned crabs for supper, of course; but lunch, which was whenever anyone wandered in between noon and five, was do-it-yourself-sandwiches and potato salad.

With those under my belt as I moseyed down the road of life, I was ruined to lesser meals; and twenty or so years later when Sister Skits and her husband Jack moved to an apartment* in Portsmouth that had its own distinguished neighborhood deli, husband Robert and I looked forward with great anticipation to their dinner invitations. We would rather have had that deli spread than filet mignon…

These days the deli tradition still runs strong. For the family reunion, Sister Skits always brings the cold cuts. Arrayed in glorious variety on the kitchen island, it's a spread that would make a grown man cry. It reduced even my spouse, the normally decisive Robert, to a quivering mass of happy indecision.

For some years at our Fourth of July reunions he stood for so long at the smorgasbord, hogging it all while he tried to decide as the rest of us waited in line salivating, that we finally, literally, voted him off the kitchen island….

He had lost his first-in-line status.at the deli spread.

Some folks will remember Foxfire's Fourths of July for the barbeque, for many years a home (next-door) grown pig roasted to (mostly) perfection on a cooker that looked like a smoking UFO; some will remember the music, or the thunderstorms… but for my children and their children, I expect their memories of family, friends, and good times will be interwoven with the aroma of room-temperature Swiss, pastrami, nickel pickles and pumpernickel, just as my memories are…

In an effort to bring some of this into the everyday, I always try to keep some cold cuts on hand for lunch, and most days that's what I have, and they fill the need; but they aren't the real deli goods. They're pre-sliced, vacuum packed, and preserved unto everlasting life (unless you buy into that too much and think you can forget about them… they will eventually go the way of all flesh)… and the quality is good, if a little "vanilla". Still, nice to be able to enjoy even a weak imitation of the Real Spread without having to wait for the Fourth of July.

That's what I was thinking several years back when I fixed my lunchtime sandwich of Swiss, pastrami, mayo, a fresh kosher dill with lettuce, and rared back and chomped down…

Well, sometimes chewy pastrami happens…
…so I struggled down the first bite and got a second.
Wow… must have been some tough old cow!

Finally, when my sandwich seemed to be getting chewier and chewier, and the first half was nearly gone, I opened up the remains to grab what was left of the pastrami and pitch it and discovered that some dastardly devil had put paper on my cheese, stuck tight to the underside. Of course, there wasn't much of it left, but what there was bore as clear an impression of my slight overbite as any dentist could wish for…

It took two such incidents to make me a really conscientious cheese-checker, and once when they switched to half-pieces of paper I missed it and had kosher paper sandwich again.

The cheese-paper innovation in packaging first arrived in boom times. The cutback to half piece of paper must have been the economy going south, or perhaps a sequestering of excessive waste of cheese-paper?

Pollyanna of the Day: If we have another great depression, we'll probably lose the extra chewy wood fiber cunningly concealed under our provolone. Meantime, I can make a pretty good case for the argument that innovation in packaging will do for America what lead drinking vessels did for Rome…

*Skits' and Jack's apartment in Portsmouth was the same apartment that had Jack's amazing sound system for listening to his music collection… jazz, swing, classical, folk, you name it, eclectic and marvelous. One of the more interesting features of his stereo setup was that the sound could be rigged to come on when you entered the apartment and flipped the light switch, as Skits discovered the night Jack was away and she came in to a dark house, flipped the switch, and was blown away by the cannons of the 1812 Overture at 100 or so decibels. Jack had carefully cued it up before he left …

… and yet he lived to a ripe old age!

Chapter Eight

Riding with Uncle Jim

When our great Uncle Jim (see littlest cherub in Galilee Church choir) was born his older brother looked at him, shook his head, and said "Druther had a goat"; and there were many times all thru Jim's long life that the rest of his family felt like we got one. His closest sister, closest by virtue of having lived longer than the others, observed of her brother "… he's the homeliest man I've ever seen… but he carries himself well."

And carry himself well he did, in a 1947 Chrysler, long past the Year of Our Lord 1947, or '57 for that matter. Cousin Carolyn used to let us know Uncle Jim would be picking her up to go to the store in his car "…with the lacework floor."

We kids thought it was fascinating to be able to look down at the floor and see the road going by, and we were fortunate enough to get to ride in it to school every rainy day. I never did know how Uncle Jim could figure out from his home in the next little town, (with no phone calls having been made; in those days calls were expensive, and something actually had to be happening to qualify for a phone call. Perhaps if the rain had been a hurricane…*) that we were going to arrive at school looking like a bunch of drowned rats if we didn't have a driver. Anyway, he would signal to turn in our drive and pull up at the house on his way to work at the Post Office, have a swallow of coffee time permitting, then drive us slowly and with great dignity the five city blocks to school, signal blinker still flashing the entire way and water splashing merrily up thru the lacework floorboards.

*Or if his favorite show Lawrence Welk was on TV. Jim always called us for that, and four out of five of us would emit a collective groan.

We didn't get rides home. Uncle Jim was still at work, and anyhow, it was okay to come home looking like a drowned rat...

Once in a while, for one reason or another, we'd ride in Uncle Jim's car in nice weather, and that was when travel with him became hazardous. In nice weather we weren't just avoiding rain, we were Going Somewhere, windows rolled down, usually on the open highway at 45 mph or (gasp) more. Under these conditions, the person sitting behind Jim had to be the fastest and most agile of the passengers, because every now and then, without any warning at all, Uncle Jim would rear back and spit right out the window and yes, into the wind. Today, thanks to Jim Croce, we all know not to tug on Superman's cape or spit into the wind; but to Croce-deprived generations, it was all in being vigilant and quick to duck.

I have mentioned this to many of my peers over the years, and have concluded that a whole generation of us was traumatized by that first generation of tobacco spitting drivers. I expect it made us better than most at ducking and dodging (good training for the politically bent); and also quick to get dibs on the front passenger seat; but I can't help but wonder about the rest of the story. When air-conditioned vehicles became the norm, did that whole generation of trauma-inducers become the traumatized? Did they just haul off and spit anyway, as they were wont to do, only to discover that the window was rolled shut? I like to think so...

Much of the lacework in Uncle Jim's car can be attributed to his love for taking it "down the Beach". In the late forties and fifties it was possible and legal for us to drive on the beach from Virginia Beach to Nag's Head, time and tides permitting; and if they didn't permit, and the tide came in before we were out of its way, an overnight stay at the Little Island Coast Guard Station was in order. Uncle Jim seemed to know every one of the coast guardsmen, most of whom were named Malbon or Midgett in those days.

Once he took the old Chrysler all the way to Ocracoke, telling the family he'd been 75 miles down the beach and 150 miles up and down bouncing over the dunes. He always loved visiting the folks of Knotts Island, famous for yaupon holly and lemon figs, who had their own delightful dialect, one piece of which I have clung to as being so descriptive of a particular kind of soul that it just can't be improved upon… that is, describing a hateful person as "… meaner i'God than a striped snake", and that's strip-ed with the full two syllables.

Could you get meaner than that?

Uncle Jim was still carrying himself well right up until he left us. He was in his seventies, and we began getting concerned when two of his lady-friends called looking for him…

He was first in our family to try out that new-fangled thing, the air conditioner. He installed it in his bedroom along with the dark green shades, which were always pulled down. When he proudly showed it to his sister, she announced that it was so cold and dark in there she felt she should have a tag on her toe.

And that's where we found him, tag-less and pre-chilled.

Chapter Nine

Horse

While on the subject of post WWII vehicles…

1946 was when folks could once again buy bicycles, yes, and automobiles, too. My family ran to teachers, tobacco salesmen, and the occasional postal worker, and while WWII had given teachers like my Mother mixed level classes of 50 or more pupils, it had been good for the tobacco industry; thus it seemed a good time for my grandfather, a tobacco sales rep for a large part of Eastern Virginia, to invest in a brand spanking new automobile.

Even just in looking at a picture of my Grandfather, it was evident that "wild and crazy guy" was neither part of his language nor his universe. When it came time to shop for good beds for my older sister and me, the salesman gave him a price, and when our Grandfather seemed reluctant, the salesman offered to drop the price, upon which my Grandfather left the store saying that if the beds weren't worth what the salesman had first asked, how could he be sure they were worth the second price?

(One absolute for these beds was that they had to be good and firm for young growing backs, so we'd grow straight and tall. The quest was highly successful in this detail… my sister and I called the beds "knee-busters" on account of what happened if you tried to jump on them.)

So for his new automobile he went to the Dodge dealer, home of the solid, well-built vehicle for the solid, respectable family man and

Freemason. There were two cars on the lot, one black and one gray. After assuring himself of their roadworthiness, he turned to my sister, age 13, and asked which one she liked best. She picked the gray one and the deal was done. On the way home, he asked Sister Skits why the gray? "Because I like the red wheels!" she said… and sure enough, the gray bankers' special car sported perfectly beautiful, almost— but not quite— frivolous, bright red wheels!

We named The Dodge "Horse" and it was beloved by all. It traveled many, many miles with my salesman- grandfather, all over his tobacco territory… and on weekends did double duty taking us all for the Sunday rides and crabbing trips that were part of America's fabric then.

Chapter Ten

Jack (Bill, Red, Son) Hayes

Cousin Jack was the son and third child of Ruth Bailey (ref. Galilee choir photo) and Judge Eugene Gresham, and was originally named Jonathan which is how he came to be called Jack. His parents divorced when he was an infant, and in the way of family-looks-after-family, he was adopted by Ruth's sister (our Auntie, Lorenna in photo) and her husband Will Hayes, who renamed Jonathan "William Claiborne Hayes, ll". The couple had been childless up to that point, so of course in their eyes the sun rose and set just above young Jack's head.

He was yet another of the red-headed Baileys that seemed the default format for youngsters in our family, and the brilliant mind that led him to be one of the founding fathers in early NASA space exploration days was in boyhood full of curiosity and mischief that kept the family laughing, if a little nervously, at his escapades. On one typical day, as part of some scientific experiment I'm sure, he kept running into the kitchen from outdoors saying "I need a cup of water"… "I need another cup of water"… until eventually someone decided to see what the thirst was about and discovered that the whole back fence was afire, not that far from our back door, burning merrily away, while Jack tried manfully to douse it with yet another "cup of water". The Fire Department was called…

Toward the latter half of WWII years, Jack graduated from Maury High School in Norfolk and was accepted at Virginia Military Institute, where he started his college days. The photo below is the young "Keydet" dressed, his Mother would have declared, "fit to kill and cripple" in his impressive grey uniform.

The Keydet

Bear in mind that all this took place at the height of World War ll…

Sometime not long after young Jack entered that august institution a letter came to our house in Norfolk addressed to him. It was The Letter No One Really Wanted in those days; so his mom (Auntie) feigned ignorance of its content and put it on the mantel to be dealt with whenever his next trip home might occur… when it finally did, she casually mentioned "Son, there's a letter for you on the mantel. It's from the President…"

It said "Greetings…"

Jack had been drafted.

William Claiborne Hayes II duly reported for duty and went for basic training, where among other things, he acquired his lifelong terror of snakes. Seems during the live fire training, when it's imperative *not* to raise your head, he came face-to-face with a cottonmouth moccasin. They apparently reached détente, but ever after in any marshy or even damp venue, Jack would swear "I can feel their beady little eyes on me"; and as much as he enjoyed fishing, it was always done with the prayer that God would not send him an eel to take off the hook.

Not long after Jack entered the Army, he was found to have Hodgkin's disease, an illness that had an abysmal survival rate in those days.

He underwent surgery at Ft. Sam Houston in Texas followed by radiation at Bethesda Naval Hospital. Later, he was one of a group of twelve who underwent experimental treatments with mustard gas, an early and drastic prototype of chemotherapy.

Jack and one other of the twelve survived. He was later the subject of a medical paper documenting the miracle of his survival, and said some years later that his involvement in the space program was in some measure an effort to give back, having been given life. (His contribution to NASA was substantial; He can be seen on film at the Smithsonian as he walked across the carrier deck to greet John Glenn when he emerged from the Mercury space capsule on his completion of the first Earth orbit. Later in his long career he focused on developing practical applications for knowledge gained in space research.)

At that point we were all living both in my grandfather's house in Virginia Beach, and at Auntie's house in Norfolk, so whenever he came home from school, the Army, or the hospital, it was to us.

Coming back from Hodgkin's he was, of course, rail thin, and required long follow up treatment at Mcguire Hospital in Richmond; but as soon as he was able, it was back to VMI!

Chapter Eleven

God Bless Our Team...

Our core family of mother, great aunt, 3 sisters, a female dog, and a transient assortment of female cats would seem an unlikely trellis for such a manly and militant institution as VMI to weave its tendrils among and around, and yet VMI was a very lively interwoven part of the fabric of our lives when I was growing up.

This was more a matter of which of our beloved cousins were involved with it than of actual reverence for The Institute itself. My Mother was in fact known to wonder aloud why anyone would send a creative child to such a structured and rigid place... but she was speaking of the impersonal gray edifice with, in her opinion, its impersonal rigid philosophy; not of "our" VMI, peopled with our beloved cousin Jack, and earlier, cousin Temple, a graduate who was already off to WWII when Jack was admitted.

Once Jack was again involved in VMI and its lively traditions, our own "Brother Rat" shared generously with the folks back home.

And so it was that during some long winter, our little tomboy sister Tobe, she of the pink flannel and eyelet lace nightgown and coonskin cap, who had requested a football and a "bonearrow" from Santa, contracted pneumonia. I believe it was over the Christmas or Thanksgiving holiday, and Tobe was to be kept quiet and rest... not easy at just below age four or thereabouts... so when Jack and his friend, in from school, and Temple, in for the holiday, got together, they volunteered to cheer her up. *

We gathered in Tobe's bedroom, the VMI contingent of three, Temple's daughter Tish, who was between Tobe and me in age; and yrs. truly; and VMI's finest proceeded to keep Tobe "quiet and rested" by telling us a few stories and teaching us some songs.

Of course, "The Spirit of VMI" was sung with greatest volume and conviction… as well as "Ollie Loves Us this we know, for the Blue Book tells us so…", a paean to the Commandant of VMI, sung to the tune of "Jesus Loves Us", which we all picked up on pretty quickly, being already familiar with the melody.

We had a wonderful time singing and listening to stories, like the one about Ole Hound Dog Jake, which I don't really remember, but do remember the adult reaction later indicating it should have had at least a PG rating.

When the evening was winding down, the grown-ups, Mom, Cousin Anne and Auntie came in to get us settled for the night. They asked if we'd had a good time and what songs had we learned?

At ages not quite four, not quite seven, and half past nine, we never ducked an opportunity to perform, so sang for them our favorite of the evening, sung to the tune of "Oh Dear, What Can the Matter Be"… continuing with…

"…Seven old ladies locked in the Lavat'ry,
they were there from Monday 'til Saturday,
Nobody knew they were there…"
then a "La de da, La de dah…" and on to the next verse…
"The first old lady Elizabeth Humphrey,
When she sat down she couldn't get her rump free..
She said I don't mind, it's really quite comfy…
And nobody knew she was there…
La de da, La de dah…
The second old lady…"

We knew all seven stanzas then and missed not a one in our recital. **

Our Auntie, present for this concert, somehow didn't get the note about Queen Victoria's passing. She would blush if any of us mentioned having a leg instead of a limb, and thighs were all but unmentionable parts of chickens; and when big sister Skits and I spent the best part of a week in our very small house proofreading a textbook for an author friend, a nifty piece of prose called "Structure and Function of the Female Anatomy", Auntie did exactly what she did during a thunderstorm... she went to bed and pulled the sheet over her face and stayed until it passed, which in the case of the book was a l-o-o-n-n-n-g time.

And now Auntie was faced with a terrible schism ... Tobe, whom she loved better than anything in the world except Jack, being taught this scandalous nonsense by none other than her precious Son.

Mom, and Anne, (Jack's sister and my godmother), also in for the serenade, were doubled over trying not to let us see how hard they were laughing, both at the three little angel songsters and at Auntie's dilemma.

Auntie finally managed a "Hrrumph!" that was as close to condemnation of the proceedings as she would manage, mustered her dignity, and left the room

I expect she went to bed and covered her head, in hopes it would all pass.

The Spirit of VMI

tune: Doxology (Old Hundredth)
Red White and Yellow floats on high
The Institute shall never die
So now Keydets, with one voice cry:
God bless our team
and V. M. I.
Amen.

*Sister Skits reminded me that this was the Christmas when parties-who-shall-remain-unnamed had brought two 5-gallon jugs of moonshine in from Florida, which probably lubricated our happily willing instructors.

**Over the years I forgot all the verses except Ms. Humphrey, probably having been intrigued that she, too, was an Elizabeth, so I recently googled "Seven Old Ladies" and sure enough, there they were in all their glory days... listed under Celtic Folk Music!?!

Chapter Twelve

Returning to the Saga of Horse, the Wheeled Wonder:

It was the wonderful old Dodge that took me on one of my favorite rides.

For several years between age eight and ten or so, I, having read Alcott's "Jo's Boys", became an avid butterfly collector.

At that age the science of it far outweighed any of the grislier aspects, and I had some quite remarkable specimens, nicely mounted on poster board. A broad network of people pitched in to contribute to my project, including some shopkeepers at Virginia Beach and the nearby hamlet of Oceana, who would call whenever a particularly choice butterfly or moth had met an unfortunate demise in their shop window. Luna, cecropia, and polyphemus moths were among my treasures, thanks to these good folks.

One summer my Cousin Jack, who had even more curiosity than I about everything under the sun, became interested in the butterflies, and asked if I'd like him to drive me to a place we called the "Narrows" (pleasanter sounding than its real name, Rainey's Gut) to try for some exciting new finds. I was in the car before he finished the sentence.

We turned into 64th Street and soon were in the wilds of 1940's Virginia Beach. The road led to the best crabbing spot around, and except for this trip, that was the only reason for being on this hard sand drive through the dunes, the pines, bayberries, hollies and scrub oaks.

Our family went there every summer, whenever there was a crowd to feed. We'd take twine, bushel baskets and crab nets, and 35¢ worth of chicken necks, and bring back a feast fit for a king.

This time though, we were out for winged game; so while Jack drove at a snail's pace down the dirt road, I sat on the right front bumper, butterfly net in hand, hoping, I suppose, for the world's dumbest member of the Lepidoptera clan to have a collision with my net.

I don't remember whether we actually caught any butterflies or not, but I'll never forget how proud I was to be sitting on the bumper with my hero of an older cousin at the wheel, on butterfly safari. All that was missing was my sash and tiara…

Another favorite memory of being "along for the ride" with Cousin Jack was the first of many evening rides in a sailboat he had built.

We lived on the Elizabeth River in Norfolk in the school months of the year and in my Grandfather's house at Virginia Beach in summer. Cousin Jack, (or Son, as his sisters called him) had built a moth-class sailboat at the house in Norfolk… He'd had a fine time in the doing of it, and once it was done, spent many happy hours on the Elizabeth River, just a stone's throw from our house.

One evening I was invited to go along on the evening sail, and at the ripe old age of 5-ish, already with major hero worship for my Cousin Jack, I was thrilled to be invited.

I got into the boat, and Jack said "Here, you hold the cat," and handed me his sister Anne's best old cat, Tom. Tom was the most docile of cats, and the two of us were long-time friends, so like the Owl and the Pussycat before us, the three of us went boating on the tranquil evening river.

After a good pull out into the water Jack said "All right, Boy, here's where you get off," and he took old Tom and put him up on a piling in the river, and said "Now let's see if he'll swim to shore".

Tom, being the kind of fellow he was, wrinkled his brow in deep cat-thought, as if studying the situation, while we slowly paddled away.

Meantime, back on the shore, Jack's sister Anne had discovered Tom was missing, and I suppose, had been sister long enough to suspect something… now she was on the shore jumping up and down and having what she herself would have described as a hissy-fit.

She was a tiny woman, like a little bird, and was jumping up and down, slapping her thigh sharply, calling "Son, you bring that cat back here right this minute!"

Jack kept slowly paddling to shore, watching old Tom, and at last Tom-the-Intrepid made his decision.

He jumped into the water and nonchalantly swam to shore as though he'd been doing it every day of his long cat life.

Anne ran to get him with open arms, and even though he was clearly none the worse for wear, she kept the hissy-fit going all the way home. Neither Jack nor Tom seemed much affected by it… like water off a cat's back, you might say… and I remember several more idyllic evening sunsets on the river "setting the cat" with Jack.

The time frame of this was very nearly the end of WWII, still a world of blackout curtains and ration books, and there was lots going on in and around Norfolk. The Elizabeth River in addition to its normal recreational uses had a fair amount of manufacturing and military traffic. The Ford plant was right across the river, and there were always barges going back and forth; and of course, the Navy and Coast Guard were ever present.

One fine day everybody trooped down to the river, Anne leading the way, thinking how fine it was that her brother at least grasped the concept of "Ladies First". (It was many years before she realized that it was not so much good etiquette as his fear of snakes in the marsh grass.)

This time it was Cousin Temple who went out in the sailboat.

He was a VMI graduate and army officer, who loved the water and had spent a lot of time on it; but somehow, conditions got out of hand, and there he was, out in the middle of the river, boat capsized…

Now it was the turn of Anne's older sister Carolyn, Temple's wife, to stand on the bank jumping up and down, shouting for someone, anyone, for God's sake, to save her husband.

Sure enough, the Coast Guard came along, just like the Mounties, and picked Temple up and brought him and the moth safely to shore.

Carolyn was so happy to have him back safe and sound that she gave the saviors the entire rum ration in joyous gratitude…

Later the *real* hissy-fit began… the one about who caused the entire week's rum ration to be given away, and whether it had in fact been worth it…

Chapter Thirteen

Motoring thru the Gene Pool

Levi Samuels

The first time I met Levi Samuels, my father-in-law to be, I had been invited to dinner and was enjoying a real Southern Baptist country meal fit for a king. Levi was a farmer, among other things, and managed one of the biggest truck farms in the state; his tiny wife Eva was an incredible cook, dedicated to keeping the engine that powered her giant of a husband well-fed and happy. If she didn't invent the "groaning board" she surely knew how to prepare one.

On the board for this occasion were fresh butterbeans, corn on the cob, and macaroni and cheese and potato salad; fresh biscuits, sliced garden tomatoes and cantaloupe… there was steak from their farm-raised beef, an inch and a half thick, cooked to perfection… and homemade lemon meringue pie, one of my all-time favorites, for dessert.

I was sixteen and slim and could eat everything with impunity, and so I did. When we had eaten, Levi looked over at me and said in his great booming voice "Betsy, do you want that last slice of pie?" Well, my Mom raised me right so I knew I should give everyone else a chance, in the certain knowledge that since I was the guest they would insist I have it. I shook my head no as unemphatically as possible.

Levi said "Well, in this house, there's the quick and the hungry!"… and polished it off without further ado.

Levi was raised in High Point North Carolina. He thought school was such a waste of time that at one point he captured and ate a large house fly in order to make himself sick enough that he could stay home from school. By sixth grade he had had enough, and so he went to work.

He had several brothers and sisters, and said later they were really poor but he never knew it because they never knew anybody lived any other way during those depression years. Levi worked in town and on local farms at first, but since his part of North Carolina was full of mill towns with goods that needed transporting up the Eastern seaboard, he wound up doing long distance trucking, primarily to the New York-New Jersey area.

He was a tall, skinny kid who never backed away from a fight, a good poker game, or any challenge; and in those hard times each day was challenge enough for most folks. For a young man on his own, with no constants, no plans, each day was to be taken as just one great adventure after another:

Levi never knew a stranger. He learned to make spaghetti from the "Eye-talians" he met in New York City, and when he'd get back home after a trip he'd invite all his friends in for a marathon poker game and Eye-talian spaghetti. Since his test for al dente was to toss the pasta at the ceiling to see if it stuck, in his bachelor days he could have survived for several days by foraging off his ceiling.

On one of his trips to New York City he met two young women who happened to mention that they had never seen stars... so an incredulous Levi drove them all the way out to the New Jersey countryside, where they got their first glimpse of the cosmos. I don't know what else transpired on that trip, but he was always proud to have been part of their education.

On yet another New York City trip he was required to get a grand piano thru a fifth story window a high-rise adventure that resulted in a back-fracture that put him in a body cast. He couldn't drive in the cast, so sawed off the leg part and headed on home.

When he was twenty eight years old he fell head over heels for Eva, a petite beauty half his age (and size). She and her siblings had been orphaned when Eva, the eldest, was twelve. Her siblings went to the orphanage, but at 12 Eva was old enough to work in the mills so she got a job doing piecework, trimming finish threads from socks. Even at that age she was a survivor, and she became incredibly fast and efficient. In later years when we would go to the garden to pick beans or some such, I would be halfway into my row and Eva at the end of hers, already headed back down the next one.

When WWII came along Uncle Sam needed EVERYBODY, so the young Samuel family added an "s" to their name and moved to Portsmouth, Virginia, where the defense industry was booming. Levi Samuels went to work in the shipyard and became a master of all trades there, and an outstanding welder.

He and Eva enrolled their first-born, Robert, in what passed for school at the time… a quickly erected Quonset hut packed with children of all ages whose families were newly arrived to serve the war cause.

It was not uncommon to have two or three grades of 50 or more children under the care of the best qualified teachers to be had, some with 2-year certificates, some with just warm bodies, doing their best to give these little people rudimentary skills in reading writing and 'rithmetic. Sometimes the little guys would get lost in the shuffle, but if they were quiet and well behaved, would be promoted to the next level. Young Robert Samuels was one of these.

As the war effort came to an end, Levi found employment as mechanic on the aforementioned huge truck farm in Virginia Beach that supplied fresh produce, kale, strawberries, corn, etc. to the same New York-New Jersey market he had known as a trucker. The farm was in what was then Princess Anne County, now part of Virginia Beach. There his gifts with machinery and his people skills resulted in his eventual promotion to farm manager.

He enjoyed building equipment for the farm; one of his home-grown designs was an implement that would renovate a strawberry field by pulling out only the plants with old roots, so the new healthy plants could move into the space. With his limited schooling he never had knowledge of drawing to scale, so drew his plans with chalk full-size on the cement floor his shop.

Meantime young Robert had reached fifth grade and was in school in the little village of Oceana, now home of the huge Naval Air Station.

The class size in his new school was down to a more manageable 35-39 pupils, and Robert's teacher, a reading specialist, noticed that as bright as he seemed to be, his reading skills were sorely lacking. She was certain given a little more time she could catch him up, so spoke to his Mother, Eva, about holding him back a year, and gave her reasons. Eva had noticed that he couldn't do his assignments, and after punishment failed to make him smarter, she was in despair, and agreed that keeping him back was in Robert's best interest.

Robert's teacher was my Mom.

He had such a crush on her he was delighted to be in her class a second time.

Mom taught in the county school and we lived in the town, so I was completely unaware of all this, and when I met Robert at 16 I was amazed to learn that he knew her and still had a bit of a crush.

My first along for the ride with Mr. S. (Levi) was an all-day fishing trip. It was more all-day getting-to-it than actually fishing, but it was quite a trip.

I don't think we passed a single little general store between home and Yorktown without stopping to get supplies and/or pass the time of day. This was when I learned that Levi's excursions, and there were many, ran on vi-ennies (the "I" in vi-ennies is the same as the eye in Eye-talian), saltines, and beer. (Vi-ennies are as important a part of real southern cuisine as Moon Pies and RC Cola. Don't knock it if you haven't tried it.)

Our first stop was to pick up a day's supply of these staffs of life... and shoot the breeze. Our next stop was to get some bait, worms to keep us going until we caught some bait fish or crab... and shoot the breeze. Then to get gas for the boat... and ... you get the idea. It took until lunchtime after our very early start to get to the fishing grounds. We put our little boat in the water and headed for a place the fish were sure to bite, the Navy's James River mothball fleet at Yorktown.

The mothball fleet was where old and retired navy vessels, or ships that might one day be returned to action, went to retire and slowly rust away. This "ghost" fleet was initiated after WWI, and at one time there were over 700 of these grey behemoths riding silently in the water near Yorktown/Ft. Eustis. (If you've never been up close and personal with our navy's warships, just imagine a New York skyscraper floating on its side... massive!)

Literature is full of reference to the feeling of awe laced with dread that goes with encountering a derelict ship. Here there were hundreds of them.

Floating around in the mothball fleet was the eeriest feeling I have ever experienced. We cut the boat motor to fish and the silence was completely overwhelming.

Our little outboard fishing boat seemed insignificant among the looming gray monoliths, and every tiny sound we made echoed off the metal around us and seemed to just deepen the silence; and curiously, the silence felt heavy, pregnant with the stories these gray giants had to tell. One could easily imagine ghost seamen aboard, miming tales of sea battles and great waves.

I was no stranger to ships and water, having a vague childhood recollection of all Virginia Beach gathered on the boardwalk to watch a U-boat burn; I'd stood on the deck of the Missouri in the spot where General Macarthur accepted the Japanese surrender; I watched the carrier Enterprise leave Hampton Roads on her maiden voyage, and was taken by launch and piped aboard ship in Norfolk harbor for dinner in my very first high heels along with my buddy and her Dad, who happened to be the ship's captain. (I couldn't believe how far up the side of the ship I had to climb to reach the deck, wobbling all the way!)

But that day in the "ghost" fleet left a memory that is as keen today as if it had just happened.

The fishermen seemed oblivious to all this. They caught enough spot and croakers for dinner, then headed for the boat ramp and home. All I felt at that moment was relief at being out from under that oppressive grey cloud... but what a profound memory to carry!

Of course we had to stop at every little general store on the way home, too, to update the grapevine on what was biting, when and where. All the way home we were reminded of why they call croakers, croakers… same reason I prefer mackerel, flounder or tuna, and that millions of folks who pride themselves on their shiny veneer of civilization don't hunt, but enjoy fishing… unlike croakers, fish, by and large, go quietly into that night…

Chapter Fourteen

Side Trip: Crabbing

…Not so with crabs. Crabs don't go silently or peacefully anywhere. They are still my favorite big game.

Most of my childhood was spent in salt water, and crabbing was a way to do that which I loved and yet be a productive member of society, not something I was accused of often at that age.

I loved the salt water, the smell of it and the taste when it dried into a white crust on sunburned shoulders… just a little on the tongue to see whether the burn was peeling or just salt.

I loved throwing the strung bait fifteen or twenty feet out and waiting for a little action, then feeling those first tentative taps on the string. The taps would grow into lengthier tugs as the customer gained confidence.

This was the time to ease the net into the water, before Mr. Crab could be seen, because if you could see him, he could see you, and it was game over. The net had to be on the side of the target zone where it wouldn't cast a shadow and spook dinner… then slowly you could start bringing him in (or hopefully, her, the sook. She'd be much fatter and tastier that her male counterpart, the jimmy.)

If you had the string in the crease of your index finger you could feel the little tugs, and try to return them, so your game would think another crab was trying to steal the bait and latch on more firmly. As she neared shore the crab would pull more steadily, trying to get back to her comfort zone, so you'd have to give just a little, playing her in.

Your hand needed to be in place on the net before you could see her clearly; too late, and she'd say "ruh-oh… outta here!" Then, the scoop… first down a tad and then up in a smooth arc, so she couldn't scale the net to escape; then quickly, the prize shaken into the bushel basket to join all the rest, who had just settled down to bubble away quietly amongst themselves only to rouse in a bizarre welcoming dance in response to the newcomer; then they'd reshuffle themselves all over before settling into their circle again.

Because we lived in a resort town, and because my Mom loved our diverse family members without reserve, our house was where everybody came for holidays and long weekends.

This could be quite a gathering, maybe fifteen or twenty people in our 5-room duplex apartment. (Rarely the upstairs apartment would be unrented and we'd use that too, but that was definitely the exception.) In our bedroom, about 12x12, my younger sister Tobe and Cousin Tish and I slept sideways on one bed and our Cousins Anne and Ray in the twin bed adjoining. The rest of the house was similarly packed, with a few hardy souls led by Tish's Dad, Temple, on air mattresses in the yard.

Auntie, who did all the cooking and was in charge of the day-to-day operation of our household, and Mother, who taught school to keep us fed and clothed, were regularly faced with the dilemma of how to feed the multitudes on teachers' pay.

To that end, Mom would give us 35 cents to buy chicken necks, and armed with those and a dozen or so lines tied to sticks, with medium weights to settle them, and a couple of bushel baskets and nets, we'd gather the usual suspects and head for the Narrows (Seashore State Park now) and a day of crabbing.

The usual suspects, because the cast of characters changed a bit from trip to trip, were:

Auntie, well-past 60, who still thought using the word leg instead of limb was too racy. (This was the same Auntie (not Ant-y) whose son Jack sent her into the liquor store for a fifth of Old Armpit, then waited with his sister in the car, both doubled over with laughter until she caught herself short at the ABC store door and came back to the car "***Son***!" After they'd gathered themselves enough to tell her what they really wanted she went back to get it, the soul of patience with all the foolishness.) Auntie wore her second best black dress for crabbing, a very wide black hat, and her oldest Enna Jetticks shoes; and she dipped the net with the best.

Usually Skits or Tish's Dad, Temple, was driving. In his quiet way, military training showing, without saying a whole lot about anything, Temple kept a chaotic world ship shape. Our lines were always in good order, and the nets mended or replaced as needed. He would usually bring a rod and reel and catch a stringer of perch while we crabbed.

When we got home he would pick some fresh mint and muddle it with sugar, crush some ice and put it in a mason jar with enough bourbon to fill it. He'd put boards on the sawhorses for a table, and spend the late afternoon cleaning fish and sipping julep, smiling to himself in his quiet way, soaking up and enjoying the craziness of the rest of his adopted-by-marriage family. Like Uncle Ray, he was family, by marriage or not.

Usually my godmother Anne, and her husband Ray would be there. Anne was as big a water-and-sunshine worshipper as I was, and really good at enticing the crabs to hang onto the chicken necks long enough to be netted. Ray would nearly always offer to net the crab and have it almost aced when it would make its getaway. Anne would slap her thigh in disgust, "Oh, Ray!"

Ray would be visibly and audibly distressed at botching the job... then someone would say "pass the net over here", Anne would set her line again, and Ray would be determined to succeed next time, only to prove yet again that he was the world's most inept crabber.

This happened often enough that once after a particularly trying day with a pup named Robbie, Rah for short, whose specialty was barking at the crabs, Auntie was heard to mumble disgustedly that she'd never go crabbing with Ray and Rah again.

Almost always along for the ride were Cousin Tish, Sister Tobe, and yours truly. If we were lucky, Mom and Sister Skits would be there but Skits was of high school/dating/job age and Mom was usually working on the Fridays or Saturdays when we needed to catch some food for the weekend.

Generally we were stuffed in one vehicle with our gear in the trunk. There was always at least one dog along, just to liven up the trip back… three wet, sandy, sunburnt, mosquito-bitten kids and at least one wet, sandy dog piling in the car with a bushel or two of crabs and three or four adults, all of us reeking of chicken necks and crabs; only one of the crowd, Auntie in her black felt hat and her Enna Jetticks, still looking dignified despite it all.

Once when we got home we found our bushel of crabs had overturned in the trunk of the car. While it's true they were trapped and couldn't go anywhere, turns out it's a heck of a lot easier to catch crabs in the water than in the trunk of a car.

Yet another time the crabs weren't biting, so we decided to "catch them with a silver hook" (we fished a lot that way, too) so we went to a place we called the crab factory, a long shed like today's chicken houses, where tables down the length of the building were lined on both sides with women whose fingers flew like magic, picking the crabs and sorting the morsels.

The detritus from this operation was discarded at water's edge, no doubt to feed more crabs (that's the kind of critters they are… "Oh, look., it's Cousin Bill! Yummy!") On this particular trip we had two dogs with us, and while we were shopping the dogs found the wonderful wasteland and rolled in it to their hearts' content. This time the crabs rode in the car with us, and the fragrant dogs rode in the trunk.

Once we were back home and several layers of swamp slime and sand rinsed off all the two legged and four legged crabbers, the venerable crab pot would come out, and in would go a little water, vinegar, salt red pepper and sometimes celery stalks and leaves… all brought to a boil before the crabs were added. They were understandably unhappy, and would try to make a break for it (as noted earlier, occasionally succeeding), but Tish's Mom, Carolyn was the quickest draw in the East with tongs and a pot lid.

Carolyn enjoyed showing folks how to mesmerize crabs so you could just pick them up with bare hands to place in the pot. This involved tapping gently but steadily on the top shell until the critter was mellowed out. Occasionally, though, one would resist and fight back, and Carolyn's red-head hot temper would address that crab with a heartfelt *ker-whack* across the beam. That ended the resistance right there…

While all this was going on, Auntie would be making the world's absolute best potato salad… NO eggs. NO sweet relish. Just potato salad the way God meant it to be…. Potatoes, onions, celery, a little vinegar, mustard, sugar and dill weed held together with Hellman's mayonnaise (we had company… had to be Hellman's. Just for us, Duke's was great.) Homemade potato salad plus a bushel of hot biscuits!

When the crabs were cool enough to handle the cleaning crew would gather to get rid of all the inedible innards and the outer shell. Mom was the lead on this operation, and it wasn't something many volunteered for. Years later, when I brought Robert home and he offered to help her clean the crabs, he was earmarked to come into the family whether he wanted to or not. (In that time no one would ever have put crabs, or shrimp for that matter, on the table for guests without "cleaning" them first.)

Then the newspaper would come out for our tablecloth, and the time-dented crab-claw-beating knives (some sterling… got to take care of the important stuff); then iced tea, potato salad, and hot biscuits by the ton. Carolyn, in charge of any food that needed the heat, would have prepared the seafood sauce. The degree of zing sometimes depended on whether she was aggravated with Temple or no, but it was always good, even if you did have to have your throat re-lined afterward.

Some of the strong iced tea brewed to accompany the meal would be on tap later for any of us who'd gotten sunburnt. We'd soak a towel in tea and dab it on the painful back and shoulders for some instant relief.

As the evening wound down the laughter and tale-telling were gradually quieter while crab-stuffed folks wandered off to find their sleeping niche. Three of us would be sideways on the bed again, trying to cool off with fans we'd made of pleated paper.

Summer days then belonged to the smell of salt air and Coppertone tanning oil; you could smell it three blocks back from the beach, at our house...

...and the nights belonged to the scent of gardenias and citronella.

Chapter Fifteen

The Fabled F-150

April 11, 2015

It's a glorious morning after a good rainy yesterday. Everything pink or gold is blooming, there's barely a cloud in the sky, and so the thing that comes to mind amid all this grandeur is… MULCH!

Just like "Time to bake the donuts" it's "time to get the mulch", and that means firing up the pickup and going to Sam Spangler's farm supply for a double scoop of brown gold.

I'm more circumspect about this pickup truck operation than in years past. It's a '79 F150 and has been fickle about firing up since it's not often used, unlike its Glory Days, when it shone in the sun like a jewel, and pulled trailers with 300 Christmas trees on board up the ess-curves of Rio Road to sell… then pulled most of them safely back down Rio when a snow and ice storm closed the business early.

Early in its career it was a brief but shining star in the big Fourth of July parade in Scottsville. For those who missed that tale, here it is:

The Parade

Fourth of July, Scottsville, Virginia
In 1979 Robert, having been promoted to the rank of major, officially

retired and began drawing his retirement check and we began selling Christmas trees in earnest, and were feeling a little flush, so bought a new tractor and the piece de resistance, a shiny new forest green F-150 pickup truck.

To gild this lily, literally, we hired the fellow who had done the gold leaf signage for several area establishments to paint on our truck around a golden evergreen "Foxfire Farm Virginia Grown Christmas Trees".

It was beautiful.

On the day of the town of Scottsville's Fourth of July festivities, where God, Mom, and Apple Pie are still alive and well, Robert agreed to take our son, my Mom (Pibbie) and Sister Skits to Scottsville to see the parade.

He pulled into town and started looking for a parking place, and the local police kept waving him on, so he followed their directions. When it was too late to back up, he was mortified to realize that they'd thought he was a float and put him in the parade.

Sister Skits, who was laughing hysterically in the back seat, told the story when they came home, saying that as they paraded through the streets of downtown Scottsville Robert shrank lower and lower in the seat until he was nearly *under* the steering wheel, while Mom was more and more into it every minute, leaning out the window waving at the crowds and urging them to "...come to Foxfire for the best Christmas tree ever..." Robert was shushing her from under the wheel, "Hush, Pibbie... shut up... oh for God's sake Pibbie, STOP IT!.."

It was Robert's first and last parade. I was just amazed they didn't win an award.

In the eighties the truck wore a big 2-canoe rack for a crown, prompting our Cousin Bailey to record a video of the rig, assuring all that Robert had a switch on the dash that would, upon arrival at the river, flip the truck upside down, so the canoes were in the water and the truck wheels up in the air...

About the time the Gilded Lettering wore off the side, when we were using about 6-10 cords of firewood a year, Robert decided to put a dump body on the WBT (world's best truck). As a full blown partner in the firewood operation, I could not have been more delighted with diamonds or pearls. I always liked stacking wood, but somehow, having to offload it from the truck was just too much of a good thing—Now life was good indeed. Everybody should own a pickup with a dump body!

After Robert was elected to the Board of Supervisors he took great joy in driving what he had now christened "my ol' rag-ass truck" to the meetings, parking it right alongside all the shiny new SUV's (bought, no doubt, as Dave Barry says, for negotiating the rough terrain in the Walmart parking lot). I could hear him coming in those nights from two or three miles away, the dump body smacking against the bed all the way down our bumpy road.

Nowadays, as I said, the old soul has a checkered history of needing a charge to start; it's speedometer kicks in when it hits a good bump; and the vicissitudes of not being driven and of old age make every planned trip a crap shoot... So it was with some trepidation that Jack Beagle and I hopped in to make our annual mulch pilgrimage.

Pushed in the clutch... yep, just as stiff as the day it was born. Pumped the gas pedal til I was tired of pumping, and then a little more... turned the key... whoom! Off we went...

Second gear, third gear, even hit fourth without grinding... It's a miracle!

Riding along on a gor-jeezus day with my best bud Jackson Beagle in the Ol' Rag-Ass Truck... What more could a girl want?

Chapter Sixteen

The Fourth

Vignettes

One:

Probably a Fourth of July, Our House, Virginia Beach...

Uncle Ray is not really related by blood. He came into the family when he married my cousin/godmother Anne; but over the years he made himself so important in all our lives that some years back at our Fourth of July family reunion we held a special adoption ceremony to seal him firmly as one of us forever.

When I was tween-age, sister Skits, six years older; and sister Tobe, six years younger; and I took turns as dishwasher every third night. The family said I washed more dishes in tears than in dishwater. Skits swore that Tobe and I plotted the year ahead so that she would get all the holiday dinners.

I've never been able to convince her that it was highly unlikely. Tobe was way too young to be involved in something that diabolical, and I was still very much in my "...just like a duck—every day's a new world..." stage. Not that I wouldn't have done it; it just never would have occurred to me to plan for tomorrow.

Anyway, it must have been a long holiday weekend because the house was full and I was washing dishes while others dried. Skits was in the kitchen too, and Tish, the cousin halfway between Tobe and me. Uncle Ray took pity on us, stuck as we were in the kitchen while everyone else was telling tales and laughing in the other room, so he perched up on the kitchen range (the only seat in our little kitchen) like some long-legged bird, and cemented his place in my heart forever when a passerby said there was still some food on one of my newly washed plates and Ray immediately said "Well, it's a damn poor dish wiper who can't get the dishes clean!"

I adored him.

Meantime cousin Temple, he of VMI military bearing and incredible good looks… a rarity among our kind… kept sticking his head in the door and chatting to keep up morale among the scullery crew. He took in the golden opportunity of Ray perched on the range and grinning a sly grin he reached a quick arm in the doorway and turned the burner on. It was a slow few minutes before we heard "Geezus!" and Ray came leaping off the range, britches smoking and long legs flailing the air and filling the kitchen with laughter.

This hub of this activity is the same 10x10 kitchen where the chef forked the defunct rat out from behind the wall for us; and the scene of my running sister Tobe's arm back thru the washer wringer when her arm got caught. It was the birthing place of a million biscuits, homemade soup and bread, tons of potato salad; and thousands of blue crabs met their demise on the same range burner that got Uncle Ray… Of course, more than a few of them escaped the pot to come sidling out from under the counter after dinner. Tish and Tobe and I would put them on strings and make pets of them, eventually putting them in the pond out back, where they came to a better, or at least more comfortable, end than a boiling pot.

Two:

New Furniture

Fourth of July, Foxfire… annual gathering of the clan site, family and friends, since 1977…

In celebration of the holiday, husband Robert invested some of his own "walking around money" in four brand new shiny plastic chairs, $4.99 a pop. He was immediately overcome with worry that someone would take his brand new chairs home at evening's end.

His Solution: take a black Sharpie and mark each chair with his initials, RWS. Satisfied, he went around back to the barbecue cooker to work on the pig.

About that time our friend "Craze" came out of the house to where we were all sitting around shooting the breeze in the yard. He took one look at the new chairs and said "Well look at that… Robert's put his name on the new chairs. He must want us all to autograph them!"

He found the Sharpie and we all spent a happy half-hour putting our names up and down the chair legs.

There were lots of us so they were well covered. It was a masterful job, and while I've never been fussy about outdoor furniture, I managed to coddle these works of art along until last year, about twenty-five years. The thought of them still makes me laugh.

Three:

The Tarp

Fourth of July, same place, different year…

Misty rain about the time the barbecue slicing began, so that Cousin Don had to hold an umbrella over Robert and Clay while they cut up the meat.

Concern over whether the skies would produce something more serious prompted Robert and able bodied assistants to suspend an enormous tarp from the branches of the maples in the yard so our guests could stay dry and enjoy the meal and music, and they did until about 10 p.m. when the bottom fell out of the sky. Six inches of rain fell in a couple of hours, sending all but the sleep-in kinfolk scurrying. The rest of us went indoors and played guitars and enjoyed our party well into the wee hours.

Next morning we were all in varying stages of recovery, heads in our coffee cups, when Robert went to the glass door and looked out at the tarp. It was so full of water it was almost touching the ground, looking like a misguided blimp had landed in the yard overnight. Without a word he went to the bedroom, came back with his pistol, shot the bejeesus out of the tarp, put the pistol away and came into the kitchen grinning, problem solved, ready for his ration of coffee and Cousin Margaret's healing biscuits.

Four:

Lock-Out

    Fourth of July, new place, different year…
We finished building our dream house. It took six years in the actual doing, and many years beyond that of planning, drawing, sawing and drying wood, but at last it was done and we moved in early in June.

I was house-proud, and ready to take the whole world on a House Tour, and with the Fourth of July Family Reunion/Block Party at hand, it was a real possibility.

Husband Robert, with six years of sweat equity invested in the House, had only one goal which was to keep the house as pristine as the day we declared it finished. Forever.

Knowing that love and loyalty would not sway her from an assigned mission, Robert locked the house the night of the gathering of family and friends, and gave sister Skits the key, with instructions not to give it to anyone, especially me, because he knew I was itching to let the people we'd known and loved for most of a lifetime go, as Robert put it,"tromping thru the house".

So they were all left wondering and locked out, not least of them Cousin Mil, who missed the briefing and having waited as long as she thought prudent, trudged all the way to the house to use the restroom only to find there was no entry.

Future Fourths, after Mil had discussed it several times in exquisite detail with Robert, there was always one unlocked door, and Skits, once keeper of the Key, was instead put in charge of Restroom Signage, so that each turn had an appropriate directional arrow to keep strays on the straight and narrow path thru the house to the potty.

Skits was delighted… turns out that was the Fourth when everybody drank lemonade, and she wound up, key in hand, three times fetching 2-gallon buckets of water from the locked house to the picnic area a hundred yards away.

Five:

The Shawl

Fourth of July Eve, old house, ca. 1984…

It was the night the Over-the-Hill Gang held forth each year. Most of the relatives and over-nighters were gathered, catching up on the years' news and swappin' tales, sitting in a yard circle that expanded and contracted as folks came and went, or on the porch. There were always some of us guitar pickers around… not the "pros", our wonderful neighborhood band… just a pick-up bunch in house, usually me, daughter Amy, Cousin Clay and our adopted Albemarle Bailey, David. Amy and I were long on the singing, and Clay and David actually knew something about playing, so it was a good match. We covered everything from Neil Young to Emmylou to Croce, from Dylan to, yes, Sousa, from Baez to the Kingston Trio, and much of the hymnal. There was always plenty of encouragement from the friends and relations gathered, and requests for everything under the sun. Fortunately, as the evening and Skits' mint juleps went on, it became less and less important whether we actually knew the song…

My Mom, called Pibbie by friends and family, had raised three daughters and retired from a long career of teaching adolescents, and neither felt obliged to suffer fools gladly or to be bound by society's foibles. On this particular Fourth of July Eve the night grew cool, and Mom went in the house to find the wonderful shawl she kept on hand for such emergencies. In the kitchen she ran into Cousin Clay, who asked what she was looking for. She said "I'm looking for my old shawl…"

Clay said "Well I'm looking for some Scotch," and opening the door under the sink said, "And *there it is!*"

Mom said "To hell with the shawl!"

Clay still raises a glass of 'Old Shawl' occasionally in honor of Mom.

Six:

It was on this or another Eve that our friend Ernie, on shore duty at Patuxent River Navy Base showed up at midnight with a bushel of fresh caught Maryland blue crabs, still kicking noisily in the basket.

The Over the Hill Gang was in rare form, it being midnight, but blue crabs wait for no man, so sister Skits and I needed to cook them. I asked David to take charge of the OTH Gang, and as I was walking toward the kitchen I heard Cousin Bailey say "David, can you play the "Battle Hymn of the Republic" for us?" David, with his usual modesty, said "Well, I can play it as good as I could all the others…", and from the kitchen I heard him holding forth, even through that last stirring verse. For once I was delighted to be on kitchen duty…

Remembrance...

In honor of our Fortieth Fourth Celebration I sent out a request for a few memories of those gatherings. The replies were heartfelt and heartwarming:

I'm not sure why Clay sent this to me instead of you although I did contact all the family to ask them to think about sending you messages as part of the celebration. Now I'm glad he sent it to me so I could see his beautiful words. My eyes are full to running over and I think he is something special.
Love, Skitsy

From Cousin Clay:

Dear Betsy,

Forty years of the Fourth. Dang! Who knew?
Most of the role models and anchors in my life were family attending the Foxfire reunions.
All were formative times in my life. Foxfire has always been a place where we could share anything from politics to family issues without fear of ostracism. We could lift up each other and provide emotional and loving support. Many confidentialities were openly exchanged that otherwise would have been concealed in other environments.
There were also times where plain old common sense and pragmatic thinking were modeled. These moments usually emanated from the familial engineering minds and/or those who attended the School of Hard Knocks.
Alcohol was never involved.*
Foxfire has always been a place of love. I've told you many times a piece of my heart resides there. I thank you and Robert for always being willing to share your farm and your love with me and my family. Our love from all of us to you.

Clay
imbibed for medicinal purposes only, I'm sure

Replies from the internet:

Karen
June 20 at 6:08pm ·
I remember our first fourth-- we were invited by friends (1988). Had a great time! Remember other friends with a new baby, the little one crawling around on a blanket by us. At another gathering, you had crabs in ice in a claw footed tub. Our daughter, Sasha, stayed by that tub eating crabs for ever!

Elizabeth Samuels Come on back! 6:30 July First... BBQ, music, your covered dish! Thanks for writing—

Carolyn
June 12 at 4:58pm ·
As of now there will be four from up here. I will give some thought to your request. I wish I had pictures of when Bobby, Vernon, Tommy and some others use to play the music. It was the best, good times.

Tish Fones
June 12 at 3:56pm · I remember so many happy times on the 4th, and most of them have to do with my wayward son, who loved to get into adult like mischief when we were there, much to the delight of my wayward family, especially Mr. Clay!!!

Amy Samuels-Arcand
16 hrs ·
Raisin Man!* He was certainly the life of the party!! (I also remember leaning on the speakers in the early days because it would make our bones hum. Aaaand sneaking... beer I now realize no one really cared if we had). I loved the 4th so much my current living situation is like a perpetual 4th. Wish I could make this one.

*An inflatable three foot tall "Heard-It-Thru-the-Grapevine" Raisin, brought to the gathering by friend Lee.

Jessica
June 28 at 8:34am ·
I think I have been to every one except maybe 2. Loved when Bobby and Vernon played, and the rope swing at the old house.

Koral replied to her comment on your post:
Wow, so many great memories, Lead baby, hat contests, good food, good music (the Snoddy Bros band), Betsy playing the guitar and singing Froggy went-a-Courtin.

The two memories that stick out most in my mind are when I found the Waterwheel* - I was soooo excited, I still have one of the paddles.

The other one is when we took Raisin man and floated down the river on inner tubes. The water was so low, that we were dragging bottom (and bottoms), so we had to wade from time-to-time - dragging Raisin Man behind. When we got back, and the sun had set Uncle Ray pointed up the hill and said "They're here. After dark they come down from the hills." We all looked up the hill, and agreed that we could see them coming down the hill, too. We didn't know who "They" were—Uncle Ray didn't say—but we were convinced we saw them ... the next morning, not so much. We also talked about putting a Foxfire float in the Scottsville parade, and dressing-up like Christmas Trees. That would have been fun, too.

*this was the mill stone and wheel that our "Mill Creek" was named for.

From Joe:
Foxfire Christmas Tree Farm 4th of July Celebration
Some of the fondest memories of my youth are from the annual 4th of July celebration held at Foxfire. I remember the pig roast. I remember Dad playing music. We played on the tire swing attached to that huge tree in the front yard. None of these compares to the memories of water balloon "wars" and playing with family and friends.

In those days our older family members that we loved dearly, were there. Most of them are no longer with us. I think of those days of fun, play, and loved ones and I...smile! What a wonderful time it was, and still is! Now, for me, it's a time to connect and reconnect with beloved friends and family. I truly look forward to it.

Joe Snoddy

One of 40 Fourth of July Invitations to Foxfire

From Ned May:

When I think of a Fourth of July celebration at Foxfire Farm, I picture fireflies cruising low over the lawn with fragrant flowerbeds beyond them and trees in the background growing dim as the dusk gathers.

I see little children among the fireflies running back and forth between blankets on the ground and groups of people sitting on chairs. How could those kids be so young? Some of them (my son among them) are grown and on their own now.

I see a canopy next to the house with a cornucopia of delicious food and drink on tables beneath it. Some of the little ones are there, poking their fingers into the desserts. Beer, wine, and sodas are in nearby coolers full of ice. Betsy and Robert are standing there greeting new arrivals and pointing them in the direction of various delicacies.

The evening deepens. The trees drop back to become silhouettes against a starry summer sky. The fireflies rise higher, blinking against the darkness of the trees. The band starts setting up on a flatbed wagon not far from the deck. Not long afterwards, the music begins.

That's the best part for me, because I love music so much. Boogie-woogie, blues, country, bluegrass—the works; I love them all. I sit in my chair cleaning my plate with my finger and listen to everything.

During the breaks I move around and talk to people sitting on chairs on the lawn. Some of them are friends that I already know. Some of them are friends that I've met at Foxfire for the first time. And some of them are old folks who come every year with their children and grandchildren. Not everyone in that last group is still with us, but I remember them. They live on in memory.

The night becomes completely dark, but the music keeps going. The older guests begin to pack up and leave. Some years Ceara and I stay until the last song and talk to the band while they take down their gear. Other years we leave while the music is still playing—more and more often as we move into the ranks of the old folks ourselves.

That's what I remember from the Foxfire Fourth. There isn't another one quite like it, not anywhere.

Ned

Post Fortieth Fourth, July 3, 2017

Happy Today! Getting back to normal (or what passes for it here at the Funny Farm), but still enough traces of a lovely Fourth to keep me smiling....

The ice cream cake I thought was a good idea melted all over its table, and while I was figuring how best to attack that, the good Lord in his infinite wisdom scheduled a rain shower and washed it off, along with my Fourth of July Salvation Army sheets that pass for table linens.... They're now hanging to dry. Still have several bottles of wine, two open on the deck, and about two gallons of lemonade. Perhaps He will send a host of thirsty Cherubim and Seraphim to take care of that...

The beautiful pink echinacea Kathy G. gave me is blooming, along with the Dame de Coeur, Lonestar and Iceberg roses; and Kathy D.'s canna which looks like the Spirit of VMI personified, is opening as we speak. The Christmas amaryllis which never blooms at Christmas is glorious, and Madonna lilies are about to pop, even tho' the rat b#&%$ deer ate my Casablanca lily buds again.... Hay wagons are rolling thru my yard...

It's all good...

PART TWO

Housekeeping 101

Chapter Seventeen

Adventures in Housekeeping

Almost from infancy it was clear to all who knew me that I was never going to win prizes for housekeeping. I always fancied myself an artist of one kind or another, so when I found the wonderful observation that "art is an attempt to bring order out of chaos…" I knew that my ineptitude as a house-person was just my way of creating the chaos necessary for art to thrive.

I never ran this by long suffering Sister Skits, who endured sharing a 10 x10 bedroom with me, my mythic pile of clothes (why would you hang them if you're just going to use them again?), and for some years a monstrous four foot teddy bear won at a carnival by a sharpshooting boyfriend.

Skits would not have been moved by my new-found existentialism. She was, I'm sure, too busy getting ready for work in her starched white nurses' uniform, then fixing *my* breakfast *and* lunch so I could ride to work in *her* car with her, then take *her* car to go to my classes at what is now ODU, where once on campus I'd leave the lovingly crafted sandwich in the glove box in the hot, treeless parking lot all day: tuna, peanut butter, whatever… then when my late day break came I'd sit in the car and eat my sandwich.

Later, on the trip home, I'd give Skits a hard time about mashing my sandwich so hard when she cut it in two I could have gotten finger prints off it.

I still don't know why she let me live.

In my domestic haplessness, I have more than once turned for advice to this paragon of domestic wisdom…

Ode (and owed) to Martha Stewart

Once upon a noonday dreary while I pondered worn and weary
O'er a mountain of upholstery stained it seemed beyond repair
Came the mailman with a "thank you for subscribing to my mag"
and a list of stain removers, saying Betsy, don't despair…
So I took my magic cloth and a big jug of white vinegar,
and rubbed those rascals briskly with a bucketful of doubt,
And miracle of miracles, just as Martha promised
those everlovin' stains came out!

Problems solved excepting one, and that one is ridickolas…
A Raven stomping thru the house saying
"This whole place smells pickelous!"

Chapter Eighteen

Blowing Snow

When I was mid-teens the division of labor amongst us kids was according to talents and general "flakiness", for want of a better word. I got to help take out garbage and hang clothes, but on account of the "flaky" quotient, I think, was not assigned things like mowing the grass or running the old-timey wringer washer. These fell to little Sister Tobe.

Tobe and Auntie together ran the wringer washer for all our laundry, and on one otherwise fine day, I heard Auntie frantically calling for help. When I went to investigate I found Auntie in a state of near hysteria, and Tobe waiting patiently and probably painfully, though she never said, with her arm caught up to her elbow in the washer wringer.

Now, the only control on the washer I knew anything about was NOT the RELEASE lever on the wringer. It was the "REVERSE" lever on the side of the machine; and on the theory that desperate times do call for desperate measures, I pulled that lever, and Tobe's arm came rolling back out.

It was a little blue, but thank heaven, undamaged, despite its two-way trip through the wringer and back; but the friendship ring on her pretty ring finger was mashed flat as a pancake and had to be pried off.

The following is a Facebook dialog with friends that will give the reader an even better grasp on how in character it is that I could have run Sister Tobe's arm back through the wringer washer.

It's a gift.

Elizabeth Samuels:

Hey ever'body... not only is the leafblower the best way to clean out your car, it's a heck of a snowblower for powder like we're having tonight! If I had a long enough extension cord, I could blow snow four miles out to the hard surface road... my cord only reaches my deck and driveway pad and steps, but that's enough for now, and the birds love it....

Beth: I'll have to remember that.
Janet: I love how you think, Ms. Snowblower!
7 hrs · Like

Elizabeth Samuels: 6 hrs. ·

Caveat! Just lost my second set of pajama bottoms to the leaf blower; one in Fall of 2013, one this morning... and these were brand new!
Janet: Do we want to know HOW ?
Joan: What in the world!?!? LOL

Elizabeth Samuels:

Well... it blows on one end, and sucks on the other... and it blows powerfully, ergo...
Just don't get carried away and try to let the weight ride on your thigh
X-Chin: Sucked up my Carharts... it's kinda dangerous... if you had a tail like a cat it could be disastrous.

Elizabeth Samuels: reply to X-Chin... Used to... Alas, no more...

Rita: I wonder what will go next??????
Greg: Yesterday you had me seriously considering getting one to save time cleaning out my car, but I will have to re-evaluate now that this safety concern has been raised.

Elizabeth Samuels: Not to worry, Greg... strictly operator error... Caught up in the beauty of the swirling snow and forgot to watch my britches! There's a moral there somewhere...

3 hrs · Like · 2
Brenda: LOL!!
6 mins · Like

Elizabeth Samuels: 1 hr ·

I put Jack Beagle out in the yard on his 75' string, finished my little bit of shoveling and came in the house and took off all my snow regalia.... Heard Jack out in the yard at the last reach of his rope, wrapped around a tree. I yelled across the snowy steppe "Go back the other way, Jack!" every way I knew to say it... Finally I put on my crocs and waded thru the snow, unwrapped him, and said "... and I thought you were a SMART dog!"

He looked at me and his body language spoke volumes:
"... at least *I'm* sleeping in my same pajamas tonight!"

Joan: You make me laugh out loud! Have loved your posts... humorous and just what I need in this dreary, cold weather!
1 hr · Unlike · 1

Elizabeth Samuels: Thanks, Joanie!

1 hr · Like · 1
Rita: Is this going to be a new show on TV?
11 mins · Unlike · 1

Elizabeth Samuels: Me standing on my snowy deck, in my state of dishabille, leafblower in hand and dog on a string? Miley Cyrus, eat your heart out....

Brenda: Love these posts'. Have read them to my family! 6 mins · Unlike ·

Chapter Nineteen

Mud Flap

Over the years mice have done a many, many dollars in damage to my shop and my garage, to say nothing of eating wires from under our cars and refrigerators; so I'm rather like Bill Murray in "Caddy Shack" when it comes to the little varmints.

Therefore it came as a matter of no small satisfaction that when I was waiting for service at the farm supply store with a nice gentleman, he called my attention to my back fender saying "Well, I've never seen one like that before!" After trying unsuccessfully to knock it off my car and finding it stuck like glue, my newfound friend announced "You got yourself a mudflap!" and chuckled.

I went around the car to take a look at what had delighted him so.

Apparently, in one of my trips through the Christmas tree fields, this young country mouse had decided to hitch a ride… and missed! A branch hit him, pretty hard it would seem, and there he was, stuck like glue, dangling from to my back bumper.

It's been two weeks now. He's been all the way to Richmond for a family get together and back in the rain to Foxfire and he's still stuck.

I'm leaving him as a warning to others in the family mus rusticana:

Look, boys, the score is Betsy 1, Mouse 0. Read it and weep....

Chapter Twenty

And So She Rode Her Damp Mop Off Into the Sunset...

No one ever nominated me for Housekeeper of the Year and I have no regrets about that.

I am not of interest to the Health Department, but if you like clutter and dust, drop by. Once when I came in from shopping with the big news that I'd bought a new dustpan my husband said "Did this one come with instructions?"

[see sidebar 1 re: dustpans]

I do like reasonably clean floors but in recent years have had a string of damp mops that:

- are expensive... a sponge on a stick, $15?!?;
- disintegrate after 2 uses into shreds that even the vacuum won't pick up, leaving the mop's sharp metal underpinnings to scrape the finish from the lovely hardwood floor.

Whenever this happens, and I prepare to replace the sponge, that's when I find that none of the refills I own, even those with the same brand name, fit the model I have.

I have seven of these misfits now. I'd throw them away, but eventually, I'm bound to buy the matching mop again, right? The odds are steadily improving! As a result I've had to dedicate some of my precious storage space to save all the refills I've bought that don't fit anything, so I won't have wasted the $4.50 per refill.

In the grocery store a couple of weeks ago I spotted the brand damp mop I grew up with, the brand that managed to maintain order over the years in our five-room apartment of five women, a dog, and miscellaneous itinerant cats. I never remember our replacing it, and only rarely did we replace the sponge, which simply screwed off, screwed on, a wonder of simplicity and reliability.

I grabbed that mop and brought it home, and waited for the cleaning urge to come over me.

Yesterday it did.

Time to break out the new mop. Of course, it came with a tight plastic cover wrapped around the business end, so I turned it end up to rip the cover off... and *there were instructions for doing that!*

In all but inscrutable letters on plastic the instructions said stand the mop on end with the sponge facing you and press down on the grooved section of the handle. I did as directed, firmly, with my strong right hand...

Nothing happened.

I then added the secret weapon, the guitar-neck gripping left hand.

Still nothing!

I stood over it and gave it all I had, and the "release" that was supposed to happen was still a non-event.

By now I knew that it would take two weeks of hard-to-come-by TLC to get the pain out of my arthritic right hand from this exercise in futility. Along with this realization came the revelation that right in front of my nose (literally, the mop and I, nose-to-nose) was the message "Questions? Call 1-800-xxxx".

Oboy

Robert Ruark once titled a great magazine article "Nothing Works and Nobody Gives a Damn", and then put tape over the blinking LEDs on his VCR. I always loved his work and felt he left us way too soon. I think if he'd lived long enough to have arthritis he'd have reached that state of grace where a "Questions? Call 1-800-xxxx" was an open invitation to by golly *make* someone give a damn! What else are you gonna do? Your hand hurts too much to do anything but read and chomp on NSAIDs. You've got the time…Make somebody else feel your pain!

So I dialed and waited mop in hand while we climbed the phone tree to the help line.

A lovely voice asked what she could do for me.

I explained that no matter how I pushed and pulled, even with both hands, I couldn't get the mop to release the sponge to get the plastic wrapper off.

She said "Try pressing very hard with both hands." I said "Hold on a sec", and gave it another big try, then told her "Nope, no luck."

She said "**What you must do is go where your floor has carpet and hold on with both hands and strike the mop hard against the floor**".

I said "Hold on a sec" again, went into an adjoining room and whaled the bejeezus out of the thing, then came back and said "No luck again".

She said "**Did you strike it really hard? Most people don't strike it hard enough**".

Whoa!

Are you noticing something here? She has enough knowledge of this problem that she knows *most people don't strike it hard enough!?* How many millions of us have called? And they're still *making* this product!?! Without even the tiny instruction to

<small>whale the bejeezus out of it on a carpeted floor so you don't destroy your moppable floor's surface?!?</small>

I explained in my best Ma Bell-trained telephone voice to this Lovely *[see sidebar 2]* that it would be a couple of weeks before my hand would be back to normal, and that there were a lot of folks in that same boat with me these days, all of us rowing in circles on account of the one hand thing; and that the company might do better to consider its customer base before its bottom line, that being the better route to lasting success.

She, of course, said thank you for calling.

About now I realized that the last Herculean blow had in fact released the sponge (and wrapper). I took the wrapper off and put it in the trash, then tried to put the sponge back in the working position. Of course, it kept falling back out... again... and again...so I fished the wrapper out of the trash looking for grace and salvation and read

to reinsert sponge follow instructions in reverse.

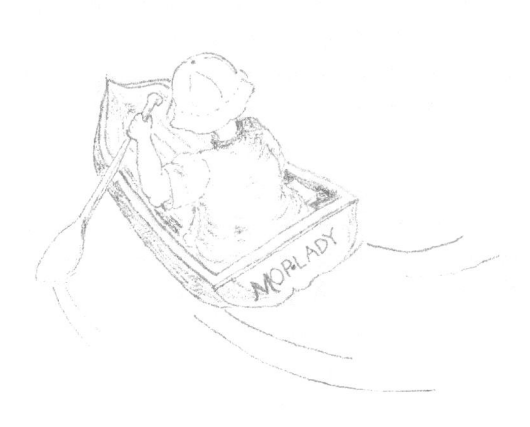

Side bar the first: Re dustpans: At least 80% of dust pans have a ridge about half an inch from the business edge that is tall enough to throw what you're trying to get into the dustpan right back out on the floor. That doesn't work, never has, never will. So why do they make 'em? To sell more dustpans, I suppose...

Side bar the second: Re Lovelies: My sister's deadly descriptive name for those generally of the female persuasion who travel thru life with perennially immaculate manicures and minds unsullied by information of any kind.; syn. sweet young things. Bless their hearts...In all fairness though, this one was doing a good job of her job... It's the management that was out to lunch.

Afterword: I have found that I can mop with this baby if when it comes time to wring it out I sit in a chair by the bucket and use one foot on either side of the flange to press the flange down thereby squeezing the water out.

I probably won't be buying another of these any time soon. After all, I finally got smart and bought the matching refill when I bought the mop.

Chapter Twenty-One

House Vac Heart Attack

As the man said... "Ho ho, good deal, Lucille..."

Working diligently at cleaning house after a four month hiatus, enjoying the whole-house vacuum, always with the "What if?" in the back of my mind that strikes terror into the heart.... That's the one where you're seeing the contractors rip out sheet after sheet of drywall to try to find where that ping pong ball wrapped in cat hair got stuck in the whole-house vacuum system.

And at just that moment, it happened. A hoodie string, about 30" long went Zup! and disappeared into my vacuum system, and the vac went immediately from a roar to a whimper, suck-wise.

I plugged the hose in each downstairs outlet with the same pitiful result, so I did what any red-blooded American would do: I made a cup of coffee and sat down to think about it.

It wasn't long before I remembered that the folks on the Internet might have some answers (they have fixed my computer, washer, and tractor in past times of distress). In a very short time, after watching a fine video, short on plot, but long on data, I decided to do what the man said and drop a nickel in the hose and see if it came out the other end, which would be the worst of all scenarios, placing the clog spot behind the wall. I added one variation to the nickel drop, which was a small but heartfelt prayer.

Sure 'nuff, the nickel went 5" and quit, and after a ten minute session with needle nose pliers and a long-ish screwdriver, I had a grand assortment of papers, pine needles and pet hair bound eternally by my hoodie string to show for my effort.

I threw the string in the trash (which I should have done when it first came out of the hoodie.... I knew I was never going to fix it) along with the rest of the debris... Fired up the vac, and it was rarin' to go, good as new....

Finished up the project with a thank you to the powers in cyberspace and to the Good Lord for keeping my drywall intact for another day.

(Note: I should mention that the Web also has solutions less drastic than drywall removal if the case is dire. They're somewhat more complicated than the nickel solution, but a long way from tearing your house apart.)

Chapter Twenty-Two

News from El Rancho de los Ratons

With a Nod to Los Serpientes

As a kid my late husband earned his spending money by running a trap line, ten or fifteen traps, to catch mainly muskrats, sometimes beavers, and occasionally a mink. He'd cure the pelts, sell them, and get enough money to keep him in .22 ammunition so he could hunt squirrels for the pot, which his Mom would turn into biscuits and squirrel gravy, the mention of which brings tears to the eyes of even *grown* boys lucky enough to have moms who can do that.

The best part about Robert's trap line was the time he spent alone in the woods, getting to know all the wild things and all their habits. Over the years this translated into an amazing body of knowledge of and respect for the wild creatures of the Earth. It also engrained in him a determination and wily ability to outwit the varmints of the world, even if the battle of wits occasionally reached bizarre levels.

Robert despised mice. When the weather got cold they would move in and, not content with being warm and dry, eat the wires of the tractor or spare car or refrigerator; and that done, eat the manuals he might have used to repair them.

To that end he spent many a winter day humming and grinning diabolically while he devised Rube Goldberg mousetraps. The most elaborate of these involved a 5-gal bucket filled with 2 gallons of water. There was a stick to climb up, and a second carefully weighted and balanced stick on the bucket rim, (a plank to walk, as it were), with a schmear of peanut butter on the far end.

Using this model he set up a 7-bucket trap line, and on a fine winter day loved to make his rounds and collect his drowned rats. Robert often saved his deer hides and had coats and gloves and purses made… I was anticipating a neatly tanned, sueded mouse-pelt change purse, or maybe some earmuffs for Christmas.

With Robert gone I drew the line at hauling that much water from place to place, and was pretty much grossed out at the thought of having to fish the little rascals out (Robert had bought seven sets of pancake tongs just for that purpose, but they were easily misplaced*, and when that happened, he'd just reach in the bucket and retrieve the mouse, often glove-less. Not me.)

*I can only account for two sets of tongs. Wonder who has the others… and what they're using them for….

But after a couple of years with no trap line, the mouse population reached the tipping point.

Their favorite spot is the laundry/mudroom/garage, and this year I was quite accidentally having pretty good luck using the mudroom commode for a bucket, (perhaps they missed going for a dip in the old traps?)

The commode had the advantage of a flush valve. The little guys would find bits of cat/dog food, eat until thirst set in, then, like misguided lemmings, head for the john, slip in and drown.

I quite adventitiously got four that way, and I thought I was holding them at bay; but several weeks ago I discovered they had moved into my van in the garage and done their usual nasty damage. I set a trap and declared war.

Since then I've averaged three per week in the trap, and last week invested in four more traps, trying to hold up the family tradition of Mouse Exterminator Extraordinaire.

Pride does indeed go before a fall.

A couple of days ago I left some washed clothes in the machine overnight and when I went out to put them in the dryer next morning I pulled the first shirt up and a gray streak went ripping by. He hid in another garment, so I began taking the clothes out, one piece at a time, and I carefully laid them aside for re-washing. Finally, gingerly, I pulled out the last piece. There he was, mus rusticus, looking up at me balefully, and just about as happy as I was at the state of our shared world.

You need to be aware that I am not in my element here. Even after forty years of country living I am still a city wuss in lots of ways.

When I was a girl and there was a mouse dead behind the drywall in the kitchen of our Virginia Beach home my Mom called a man who helped out around our place, who called a friend, and ultimately the chef at one of the better Virginia Beach hotels came to the door, chef's toque in place, and used his long handled kitchen fork to remove the mouse. A grateful Mom paid him handsomely and all five of us laughed until our sides hurt at the stellar culinary service.

I didn't know any chefs locally, so after mentally testing a number of solutions for getting the mouse out, none very satisfactory, I remembered I had made a smallish butterfly net for the kids. I squished it a little for a better fit, and the battle for the washer was on.

Twice I had mousie in the net, and he climbed up it so fast I had to dump him back in the washer—better there than loose—but finally he went far enough in that I could grab the net above him so he couldn't skitter out; then doing what passes for running with me these days, I ran like the wind to the deck and hurled him as far as I could in the opposite direction from the garage.

Snappy the Dog and Bill the Cat were in hot pursuit, but he made a successful escape. He had put up a good fight so he deserved a shot at a getaway. However, it was his one-time exclusion... if he comes back, I'm putting Bill the Cat in the washer with him.

Meantime, I've decided that leaving Snap the Dog's morning chow on top of the washer overnight is bad Karma. It was nice not to have to go down in the garage to get it first thing in the morning, but I'm sure I can find a workaround.

About Los Serpientes...

...same mudroom, different day...

When spring arrived and I was busy in the yard, I'd been careless about leaving the garage door open, only thinking fleetingly about my resident black snake, Big Jim, wondering if he might find the warm cement inviting with the nights still cool and the mice still in residence; but I was busy and so I ignored that wisp of wisdom until I headed down to the garage one morning and happened to glance left into the small bathroom, and there, bathing in the afore-mentioned mouse-trapping commode, was a five-foot black racer.

He saw me and pretended he wasn't there. I did the same, then said quietly to him "No need to panic... as you were, young fella." I backed slowly away, pulling the door closed. Then I put on gloves and grabbed a mop handle and slowly went back to the door, and ever so slowly moved into place. I quickly pinned the snake to the commode rim with the mop handle, grasped the big guy behind his head, and while he wrapped what seemed about 20 feet of writhing muscle around my arm, I headed for the same flower bed where I had thrown the mouse, and let him go, telling him to go in peace and never darken my mudroom again.

He wasted no time and immediately vanished into the brush.

I later decided he was not Big Jim, but perhaps a son or even granddaughter; Jim is larger. I've spotted the big guy (or gal) a couple of times since and he/she seems content in the flower bed and has a nice hole to hide in there.

What is clear and a bit worrisome to me is that this mudroom commode has apparently become known far and wide as a watering hole. These days when I go down to the mudroom I always glance left, half expecting to find a rhino or a wildebeest quenching his thirst there.

When I do spot one, he needn't expect a trip to the flower bed from me… I'm slamming the door and calling the game warden.

Chapter Twenty-Three

Country Winter

Home for me is a Christmas Tree Farm, a wonderful place we named Foxfire, not for the wonderful Foxfire books… they were a nice surprise later… but for the miasma that phosphoresces from old logs in the woods at night. Our Foxfire is on the south side of the James River in Buckingham County.

Despite being fitted with all the amenities of civilization, Foxfire still manages to keep an atmosphere of "Life on the Edge". Bears, coyotes, foxes, bobcats and even a cougar sighting once… any of these critters are apt to drift across the yard on any given day.

But the most dangerous part of Life on the Edge is Weather.

From Hurricane Camille in '69 to the second "hundred-year hurricane" three years later, to the terrible derecho just a few years ago, and then later the earthquake that cracked the shop floor, there's always excitement a heartbeat away and when least expected.

But the weather that beats all comers here is my least favorite four letter word, S-N-O-W.

If you live at the end of several miles of dirt road that is heavily wooded on both sides, you had better have several kind and able bodied neighbors to plow and chainsaw you out when the storm permits.

You will also need a plan:

Making a shoveling plan. Going for the front porch since every time I clear the back deck another two foot avalanche slides off the roof. This way I can clear around the generator and clear a small men's room for Jackson Beagle.

I have birdseed to throw out so my winged friends can help melt the residual ice while stomping around on their hot little feet as they munch on the goodies. Expect the power to go this evening with wind and a wetter snow...

OK, so I've done a test run on my generator, loaded up the gas cans in case the power goes for a couple of days, started the gas heater at the other house and made sure it was running well in case I have to go there to get warm... Now to put the Kubota somewhere that I can dig it out with the snow shovel so I can get to the other house if I need to...

Battening the hatches, Buckingham style...

Lexie-da-Cat and Jack Beagle are fed up with being weathered in so decided to have a free-for-all in the kitchen yesterday evening... one thought the other might be getting more to eat (that's what all three of us are doing to beat cabin fever— eat). I put them in time out and we all sulked. Reminded me of those times when Mom would say Sister Skits and I had to sit in chairs facing one another until we could "Say a pleasant word". Sometimes it was a l-o-o-o-n-g wait... and we found that merely spitting out "A Pleasant Word!!!" was NOT what Mom had in mind.

But we all know, thanks to Robert Burns, what happens to the best laid plans of mice and men...

All my clever organizing for the Winter emergency came to naught, thanks to "progress".

I get it that Americans are unlikely ever to see their elders as national treasures as the Japanese do. However, I do think our scale of values is a little out of whack.

Today's designers of child safety devices have become so focussed* on the below-six demographic that there are no allowances made for us folks who actually *need* to get into containers and packaging.

Case in point: I purchased new gas containers for my generator. My friend Tank filled them and put them on the porch beside the generator so I'd be ready for whatever came along.

What came along was a bitter cold snap, snow and a power outage, so there was no heat in my home. **B**ut remember, I have carefully prepared for this! Plenty of fuel, right there beside the generator!

Unfortunately, when I needed to add gas to the generator, thanks to the "improved" safety features designed into modern gas containers, there was no way I could get the gas cans open.

I got out pliers, a wrench, and a screw driver, and finally my trusty box cutter, to try and defeat these "safety" features. The plastic was so strong even the box cutter couldn't touch it.

It was nighttime, so I bundled up as warmly as possible, trying to sleep through the cold until morning. Happily it was not one of those week-long power outages.

I started to say next:"If it had been, the newspapers would have headlined '*Woman Frozen to Death; found by her generator with a box cutter in her hand* "...

But the more probable headline would have been **"Child Safety Device Works!"**

Next day the electricity was humming once again at Foxfire, and I am grateful not to be an unfortunate statistic, but it's only a matter of time until the next Polar Express.

So c'mon all you incredible, designing, keep-us-safe-from-ourselves minds! Let everybody on the bus!

After all, I can go in my local "dollar store" and for $3 buy enough junky fall-apart plastic toys to take out a boatload of kids if the toys are fallen on, ingested, or otherwise misused, and the label says only "adult supervision recommended", or "not for children under three"....

I'm jes' sayin'...

*spellcheck suggests I may wish to use "focused" or "cussed" here... Yep, I might!

Chapter Twenty-Four

While on the Subject of Good Neighbors...

Riding with Duffy

Until we bought the farm my experience with living the rural life had been pretty much limited to Sunday rides in the country with my Grandfather, who had some acreage that others farmed where we could generally get corn in season; or we might ride out to a great-uncle's place for honey. I had "helped" with growing a "Victory" garden with my godmother, Anne, long after WWll was over; and later, spent time with my husband's family, who were very serious farmers and gardeners.

At a very young age my ambition was to be a botanist, so I was really fascinated by anything to do with gardening; but real hands on country living was beyond my ken. I was always a voracious reader, though, and used the time that seemed to come in 20 minute increments when my children were small and I had no actual garden to play in to absorb every word of Rodale's Organic Gardener, Ruth Stout's mulch gardening, Taylor's Encyclopedia of Gardening, and riding the crest of the wave of the first great Green Earth movement of the 60's and 70's, the Mother Earth News, wherein I learned how to make a circular firewood stack and homemade granola, both very time consuming, but highly satisfying when done.

Since my husband had grown up on a conventional farm, milking a cow while it placidly stood on his foot, he and I had decided to raise only Christmas trees and our garden on our farm, so I really had nothing in the way of livestock experience except memories of repeatedly sliding off the back of an old mare on my father's family farm, and of once beating a very hasty retreat when confronted by one of my father-in-law's 300 lb. sows who challenged me face-to-face with a "Woof" when I headed down the lane one morning.

I still don't have much background with livestock, but I'm pretty good at picking up vibes from animals, and that old sow had trouble on her mind. I tried to make walking backward rapidly look cool and confident, and failed abysmally. The folks back at the house had a good laugh at my expense, but then, as now, I'm convinced that discretion is indeed the better part of valor, and living to fight another day is a worthy goal.

Anyhow, we moved to the country, and I was determined to demonstrate that I could cut it as one of those strong country women, like Olan in "The Good Earth", a long time heroine of mine.

I did make lots of round stacks of firewood, about 8' across and 5' high, and they were beautiful. The local copperhead population loved them.

We grew a garden and my father-in-law taught me to can, and many summer days when it was too hot to garden were spent in the kitchen canning, sans air conditioning in those days, ably abetted by my mother, herself I think a closet Olan.

The perspiration level over the canning operation was such that we didn't need to add much granular salt to the product. Sometimes in an effort to cool off we'd put cucumber peels on our foreheads and shoulders … they're wonderfully cold when first applied and they make quite a fashion statement.

Of course, the stove had to be roaring hot until the last jar was canned, usually day's end, when we would load everybody into the car (a '55 VW sunroof beetle) and drive to the creek for a cool down. By the time we returned we'd be hearing the satisfying "pop" of jars sealing.

The closest I have ever come to committing homicide was one day during a red-hot canning season when an insurance salesman came to assess our coverage, and looking at me all sweaty and covered with tomato juice and cucumber peels said "And do you work?"

I think the daggers from my sweat-befogged eyes stopped him in his tracks, because he said

"I'll put you down as 'domestic engineer'."

Anyway... when we finally moved to the farm full time, I ran headlong to embrace the country experience, so when my next door neighbor Duffy asked one hot summer day if I'd like to ride with her to pick up two live chickens at old John's farm, I said "Sure!"

She had a red Ford Fiesta, carrying capacity like a VW Beetle on steroids.

I got in the passenger seat. Her two year old nephew stood between the two front seats and operated the radio, as well as the heating and cooling controls, (seat belts and child seats were still novelty items); and her four year old daughter was in the back seat chattering away.

We set off enjoying a different radio station every few seconds and alternately being heated and cooled until we reached John's chicken houses.

The owner could only be described as a crusty fellow, but he was very fond of my neighbors, and good to share the fruits of his labors with them. He invited us into the chicken house.

I'd never seen anything like it in my life... Thousands of chickens milling around at 100 degrees, waiting to be delivered up to one of the huge chicken-processors, and probably looking forward to the ride in the cool highway breeze.

The aroma of a ripe chicken house is an unforgettable thing, and made my neighbors' hog operation seem almost pleasantly fragrant.

We waded through the teeming masses, following John, who carried a stick with a loop on the end, which turned out to be a chicken-lasso. He hunted for just the right bird (they really did look the same to me) and zup! slipped the loop around a foot as slick as anything, lassoed another, then said "One for *her* too," nodding in my general direction, then zupped up another.

He tied the three chickens' legs together with a string, and carried them to the car for us. We thanked him profusely, (me just beginning to wonder what in the hell I'd gotten myself into), and he laid them on the deck under the rear window of the Fiesta.

After the requisite exchange of pleasantries and local tidbits of gossip, we were on the road again, with the two-year old running the heater and radio; the 4-year old chattering away in the back seat; and the three chickens on the back deck, tied together at the ankle, every now and then all leaping into the air and clucking away (which sounds easy, but if you think about it, can't have been).

At this point my neighbor said "I need to stop by the pet store for a minute", so we proceeded southward to Sprouse's Corner where she pulled in at the pet shop.

She and her daughter disappeared inside, reappearing a short while later with a beer flat containing 3 guinea pigs. They more or less settled in the back seat with the four-year old, who was valiantly trying to keep them from escaping, putting toothpaste back in the tube as it were.

One more short stop for a few groceries and we were on our way home, wind in our hair, heat and radio running full blast, guinea pigs making mostly futile attempts to escape their box, and every few minutes, like some bizarre-o demonstration of synchronized swimming, three chickens clucking and leaping high in the air in entrechats that would have made Nijinsky weep with joy.

We were only about 40 minutes from home, but in the 30-odd years since, the memory of that ride has never failed to bring a grin.

Chick Ballet

My neighbor was absolutely unfazed by it all, acting as though she ferried Noah's Ark up and down the highway every day; and when we at last arrived home she headed in to put on a large kettle of water, asking if I'd like to process my chicken there, too?

My mental brakes screeched…

What? *Process my chicken?*

My whole mind went into overdrive attempting to fathom what "process your chicken" might mean, except for the 5.5% of my mind I left in charge of making sure my coolth showed that I processed chickens every day, sometimes twice on Sundays.

About this time my neighbor's husband Bob passed thru, axe in hand, headed for the back door and his two chickens. He glanced back at me and asked "Want me to kill yours for you, too?" I managed to croak "Yes, please…"

A grisly hour or so later I headed home with my trophy.

It was, in the vein of "what doesn't kill you makes you stronger", a Great Learning Experience, and I was grateful, to neighbors who could be gracious enough to show a townie the ropes without collapsing on the floor in gales of laughter; and to crusty old John for the chicken, which I kept in the freezer for nearly a year before I could make up my mind to eat it.

After all, it had been a boon traveling companion…

A little history here: when I was first married I could make coffee and soup and bake bread, and that was my entire repertoire. I had failed Spam-frying miserably by failing to rinse the soap off the frying pan the only time I was asked to try it. After that, my family found other things for me to do. (My family spent a lot of time looking for other things for me to do.)

The first time I cooked dinner for my husband, I had asked him what he'd like and he said "Fried chicken."

I had eaten a lot of it… how hard could it be? But then I realized that I would actually have to handle a raw, slimy chicken with my bare hands.

Raw chicken feels like snakes ought to feel if they really wanted to do it right.

After I had gingerly floured said fowl, I poured troop issue cottonseed oil from the commissary into our brand new wedding gift electric skillet, set, per directions on the handle, for "fry chicken=375degrees" and sat back to wait for our chicken delight. An hour later the bird was still the color and texture of raw chicken.

It was a long, long time before Robert requested fried chicken again.

Several years later he brought a couple of wild ducks home. He was an avid hunter, and our deal was if he'd clean it, I'd cook it.

I was a far more experienced cook by then, so I stuffed in some orange and put a little bacon on the breasts, and put the ducks in a hot oven in our Navy housing apartment.

Half an hour later, eye-burning smoke was pouring out of my oven, and neighbors were pouring out of the five other apartments in our building.

Turns out our perfect "you clean, I'll cook" deal made no mention of whose duty it was to cut off the feathered feet...

Chapter Twenty-Five

Continuing the Subject of Good Neighbors...

Olive

Years ago in Massachusetts I knew a remarkable lady who painted her living rooms with brown enamel, and had her husband saw the corners off their furniture so the kids, all four of them, could put their hands anywhere when they ran into the house without making a mess; and so they wouldn't crack their skulls on corners as they ran thru.

Olive had a bar built in her cellar so her husband wouldn't have to leave home nights. She got to name the street she lived on and named it a color "so they kids could learn to read and write it early". She started the house numbers at "One".

An entirely practical woman...

After we had been in Massachusetts for six months, the Air Force decided to send my husband to Germany, Spain, and ultimately, Majorca, to be a part of an over-the-horizon radar project. He had never been outside the grand old USA, so we decided that of the two of us, he would be the one most likely to need some ready cash. I had enough food on hand for my girls and me to make it until my Mom came for her visit or until payday, whichever came first.

Then I heard on the radio about the Sumner tunnel, and learned that it was on the most direct route to Logan Airport in Boston, where I would pick up Mom.

Since I really don't like tunnels and had no money at all for tunnel toll, I consulted our map for another route. The alternative I worked out was the long way 'round, in a northern loop. It looked doable but I was most fearful that I might take a wrong turn off my northern loop and wind up in the Sumner tunnel without one red cent for toll.

The old Kingston Trio song about the man named Charlie who got stuck on the Boston MTA without fare to get off at his station stuck in my head, the difference being that while both of us were flat broke, I'd have two little girls riding with me forever "through the streets of Boston", and nobody to hand me a sandwich thru the open window.

I barely knew Olive then, but knew my other neighbors less, but she seemed so kind and approachable that I mustered my courage and went across the street and, explaining my predicament, asked if she would consider lending me fifty-five cents in case I wound up at the Sumner tunnel.

Of course she would! And she'd look after the girls for me, too, while I went to the airport…

God love her… what a saint.

I made the trip without encountering the tunnel, but in my eagerness to avoid it on the trip home, I accidentally wound up in New Hampshire. I said "Mom, I'm so sorry… I took a wrong turn and we're in New Hampshire, but the sun is shining now, so I know which direction will take us home."

She said "That's what I love about riding with you. It's always an adventure… I've never been to New Hampshire before!"

Our Massachusetts garbage man raised hogs, so the weekly garbage we gave him had to be first quality swill. He spurned mine for two weeks early on because I thought hogs could eat eggshells and threw some in my bucket. Silly me!

Olive made a game in icy Massachusetts of putting out the "swill" bucket for him every Thursday.

She'd stand at the top of her downhill driveway in her big coat, galoshes and babushka, and using her broom like a hockey stick give the bucket a good shove. When it made it to the road edge on the first try she'd raise the broom in triumph.... Gretzky had nothing on her!

All Olive's kids did their own room decorations, and the daughter, after a particularly daring redo of her quarters, told me she loved it because the colors "clashed beautiful together".

Mrs. P. (Olive) kept big gallon-sized ice cream buckets with lids for the kids to stack like blocks. Two of the buckets were full of collected buttons for little people to sort and play with, or just to throw around to see how pretty they looked. She babysat my girls while I substituted at the local school, and we split the pay. I was delighted with the arrangement because I knew the size of her heart, and that my girls were in good hands.

Anyway... on a visit to my house one morning this wise woman took one scornful look at my brand of teabags and explained that if I really liked tea, I should be using *her* favorite brand.

This was 1965 and I'm still using it, in part in deference to a great character... and also because I found when I bought some, her brand is like Crackerjacks. There's a prize in every box! Always some funny little porcelain figurine, many sort of homely, many pretty cute in their own way once you figure out what they are...

So today I opened a new box and just like a kid, really couldn't wait to see what little bit of kitsch was within... This time it was a seahorse.

He will join the multitudes of earlier prizes that turn up just about anywhere in my house, things which will probably cause some consternation when I leave among those who never knew the joy of the magical tea box and the surprise therein.

Thanks, Olive, wherever you are... I hope you're still the swill-bucket champ of Littleton, Mass. But if you've gone on to glory, hope you're enjoying your very favorite R&R at the Big Demolition Derby in the Sky!

Chapter Twenty-Six

Along for the Ride...

The Volkswagen Era

In the beginning there was the Beetle:

Once our little people began to hit school age, about 1966, it was apparent that it was time for us to become a two-car family so I could get the kids to and fro. The options were limited by the military pay-scale at the time, and since lieutenants weren't very far up the ladder, our prize was a 1955 Volkswagen Beetle, $400.

It was like lots of cherished things in life, so ugly as to be beautiful… Its color was that "primer black" shade that along with "primer red" made up most of the VW palette early on. Its leather seats were stuffed with "horschair". Heating was nominal at best, though compared to the microbus we later purchased, it was warm as toast; and the air conditioning was a 4"x13" sunroof that flipped up.

The Beetle had no signal lights. Instead there were metal flippers at the front windows that were manually flipped out from the inside to let the following cars know you were turning.

Of course, the drivers of the following cars had long ago quit looking for anything but signal lights, so one had to rely on the flipper plus frantic hand waving, plus the Power of Prayer, which I especially relied upon on those rainy days when I would be entrusted with driving all the local kids to school.

The '55 also had no gas gauge, but it did have a reserve tank that was accessed by yet another flip switch, so if you accidentally ran out of gas, a flip of the switch got you another gallon, 35 miles… not too shabby!

The Bug was really nimble downhill, but could have used a bike-pedal assist along with more heartfelt prayer going uphill. It was a good idea to fly (top speed and cruising speed, 55mph) on the downhill run to get some momentum for the uphill side of a grade.

Apart from the mileage and the hippie status, the VW's greatest asset in my book was a real emergency brake, a lever you could pull up and actually use to make a controlled slowdown or to halt the vehicle. Subaru had this later as well, and it was such a practical working idea that it was only natural that it disappear in favor of an "emergency" brake that is counterintuitive to engage and requires a PhD plus a secret decoder ring to disengage.

Our apartment access in Greenbelt, Maryland was at the top of a hill, which was a big advantage in winter when the cold-natured Beetle didn't want to start. I'd put it in neutral, grab the window post and push, steering the car out of the parking slot onto the main drag. Once there, I'd give 'er a shove, and while rolling downhill, leap in the car, put the car in gear, pop the clutch, start the engine, and motor on my merry way.

I might have done as our neighbors at Washington State University did, with their classic German efficiency… on frigid mornings Friedrich would disconnect the battery, take it in his apartment and warm it in the oven, then tear out to his Beetle cradling his warm battery like a baby, reconnect, then put-put-put on to class, but:

1: the battery was the heaviest part of the VW and it was a long run to my oven; and

2: I would probably have gotten sidetracked with the kids, forgotten the battery in the oven, and blown all of us to Kingdom Come.

The drawback in my method was my own propensity for smacking my head on the door frame when leaping into the vehicle; but after a number of years with the Beetle and later the Bus (yes, more to follow) I developed a thickening of the head-bone that served me well with autos as well as later in my twenty years on our local School Board.

Our other car in these and many years to come was a red VW fast back with a little more room and a few more frills, like HEAT. It was Robert's commuter car, and our "road trip" vehicle, which included our monthly payday trip to the Fort Meade Commissary, where we would wait in the payday line to get a basket, wait in line to get in the store, wait in line to check out and head home, all four of us and enough groceries to last the month in a VW fastback.

To this day I don't know how we did that, any more than I know how when I was a youngster, we lived, all five of us women, in a house with one bathroom.

There's a Life Lesson there: Sometimes if you don't know it can't be done, you can do it.

Anyhow, on one commissary trip the produce man was unloading grapefruit and piling up for disposal the empty "orange" crates.

The thought of those wonderful do-it-yourself gold mines* being disposed of was just more than I could bear, so I asked if I might have some. "Sure lady! You can have all you want, but I have to get them out of here tomorrow…"

Next day, after the girls were in school and Robert off to work in his fastback, I was chugging up the Baltimore Washington Parkway on my way to Ft. Meade and good junk heaven. After half hour of trial and error, packing and re-packing, I managed to get five wonderful BIG orange crates in the Bug before heading home with my treasure.

That was in the Year of our Lord 1966, and all five of those crates are still in service, having been used as shelves, toy boxes, plant stands, patio furniture, shop display shelving and storage, among other things. What a Coup!

Those same orange crates were recycled by the multitudes, especially young families of limited means, for all sorts of furnishing needs. Cousin Jack, later of NASA renown, with his wife Mil had orange crate furniture liberally strewn around their starter apartment. The period? Jack called it Early Lydia Pinkham…

Chapter Twenty-Seven

The Beetle

Part the Second

After a couple of years in Greenbelt, Maryland we were finally able to get base housing, the only time in Robert's military career. It was a very important step up because military pay was not designed to cover life on the local economy in the metropolitan D.C. area.

Our new housing was in Indian Head Maryland at the Navy's Ordnance Disposal base, where brave souls from all branches of the military were trained in bomb disposal. Since these were the Viet Nam war years, Arab Israeli sniping was ongoing, and Northern Ireland bombings a daily event, training also included dealing with unconventional warfare devices— punji sticks, letter bombs, you name it— products of enormous creative power abused in designing ways to kill and maim.

The tri-service expert on foiling such devices was our next door neighbor, and when Robert was working on the Shrike/Standard Arm Missile, letter bombs had a brief but impressive run in the DC area. Our neighbor was able to give us a good briefing as to what to watch for in the mail.

This was during the time our neighbor (talk about multi-faceted) was also doing great cartoons and stories for "Grunt" magazine and carving amazing sculptures with a chain saw in the back yard, where he also walked his boa constrictor daily.*

"Grunt" was designed with the guy in the foxhole in mind. and talked of all the things he dreamed of most… women, beer, combat, women, more beer… just to name a few. Its language for that era was pretty explicit.

My creative neighbor asked if I would proofread his stories for grammar and spelling before he submitted them, and I was happy to do it.

And so it came to pass that I had a copy of "Grunt" in the house when my Mom came for a visit.

In her own personal matters, Mom was last and least a prude. Among the "momisms" she gave me to live by:

Language: If you fear a word, it controls you. Don't give it that power, just use the word appropriately;

Nudity: Let children run around without a stitch as long as possible, so they'll develop a strong sense of self;

Narrow mindedness: Don't spurn something new as bad without first trying to understand it;

In other words, think freely and let other folks do the same…

Despite these noble ideas, it was pretty clear that a lot of this liberal advice was not to be practiced by her three little girls, and certainly not when she was around. I'm sure when my children arrived she ran to the East window, looking for a star.

The star wasn't there; but the "Grunt" magazine was. There, in my house, slipped between the pages of a glossy homemaking magazine, which was of course the first thing Mom picked up to read.

The hush was deafening…

---

* Our neighbor's snake was named Heinrich originally, but changed to "Edith" after a month or so… I don't know how the disguise was unmasked, should've asked, no doubt. Edith enjoyed her daily walk in our fenced back yard and must have tasted freedom there, because we came in from shopping one fine day to discover that our neighbor had

dismantled his car in the parking lot, even taking the door liners off, all to no avail. Edith was long gone—never even sent a postcard.

Indian Head was a great place to live, and we treasured the remarkable people who came into our lives there.

Of course, our Beetle was there with us, still chugging along. It regularly plied the road from Indian Head to Andrews Air Force Base where I would take care of groceries and sometimes meet Robert for lunch at the Officers' Club. At that time he was working at Andrews Air Force Base in the Systems Command Plans Office, before moving to Crystal City to work on missiles.

Since his primary assignments had to do with engineering and contract management, these were years when he spent a week or so each month on the road, to Texas Instruments in, of course, Texas, or China Lake where the missile test range was, or visiting other contractors' sites, generally flying in and out of DC's National or Dulles Airports on the redeye. At least once every six months he would forget and leave his keys locked in his car, and I'd get a call asking me to drive to the airport, unlock the car, put his keys on top of the front tire, lock the car, and motor back to Indian Head.

I can't begin to compare my little assignment to checking out missile tests, but will posit that even in 1968, driving a '55 Beetle around the Washington Beltway was at least that exciting. I don't believe anyone, ever, has driven the Beltway as slowly as I, at fifty-five mph, my "top and cruising" speed. It was pretty much a ducking and dodging blur. There was some skill and there was a lot of prayer.

If a car failed on the Beltway and the driver went for help (nope, no cell phones back then) on returning, the owner found a derelict ship of a car, stripped of radio, tape deck, tires, and anything else removable. The Beltway and the wild, wild west were not too different, and when Robert got tired of being chased on his daily commute by carloads of pirates brandishing knives and other weapons he put a 40 millimeter flare gun under his seat and would flash it to ward off boarding parties. With close to a 2-inch bore, it did.

(He'd been given the flare gun by an old merchant mariner, and used it

for several years at the farm to celebrate his birthday, which was in February. There was usually snow on the ground, so it was reasonably safe, but after nearly setting the farm on fire a couple of times in atypical winters, he decided to sell it before it caused his worst birthday ever.)

If for any reason you had to venture around the Maryland side of the DC Beltway there was the additional challenge of the disappearing lanes. You'd be put-putting along at 55mph, in the VW zone, and suddenly, POOF! with no warning, your lane would vanish.

It could take what seemed hours to get a break in the stream and fade back out into traffic. There was, of course, the option of driving in other than the right lane, but that was not for the faint of heart or 55 mph pipsqueaks, so I'd hang to the right and pray for Virginia. I always felt like I should get out and kiss the ground on safe arrival back at Indian Head.

Thru it all the stalwart little Beetle kept on truckin', like the little engine that could. I decided to reward it with a paint job.

One of the best things that Uncle Sam ever devised for the morale of his service men and women and their families was the Base Hobby Shop. Indian Head Naval Ordnance Station had an extraordinary one.

In a time of great world tension (Viet Nam for starters) and in light of the exacting life and death jobs explosive ordnance disposal (EOD) experts had, many of Uncle Sam's very finest found a peaceful and creative haven in the Hobby Shop. There was all the materiel on hand for woodworking, auto repair, and ceramics; and tables, lockers and work space for all sorts of creative pursuits.

A neighbor married to an Army EOD man put me on to it (Uncle Sam understood that spouses were under tension, too). She had taken up ceramics, and invited me to try my hand at it, so while our kids were in school, we'd be hard at work at the Hobby Shop on projects for birthdays and Christmas for friends and family.

I really loved the smell and feel of the clay, and pouring the molds and firing them was great fun, but since someone else had made the molds, and they weren't hot from my hands off the potter's wheel, it didn't seem quite as creative a process as I wanted… putting the glaze on was mostly a matter of choosing among the glorious colors and textures, not of really "creating". Then my friend introduced me to "one-stroke" painting on greenware, unfired, still somewhat moist clay-ware, where the object is pretty much a blank canvas for painting. I had a wonderful time. The depth of the one-stroke paint on greenware was lovely.

The maestro of the Hobby Shop was expert in all the arts and crafts in his domain. He advised me about all matters to do with the firing of the ceramics, and always took great care with the things I brought for firing, even to doing a separate fire when I put gold leaf accents on a piece.

As he explained, gold leaf is a magical touch on a piece, but if it encounters any kind of dust or impurity between the time it's applied and the time it's fired it turns an unfortunate shade of magenta, completely trashing all the art, blood, sweat and tears you might have invested in the piece.

The Maestro was a man of few words of praise, but when they came they were treasures... One piece he liked especially needed all his special care in firing. It was The Twelve Days of Christmas platter I did for Mom, with the gold leaf accents. They came out of the kiln clear as a bell, no magenta... Thanks, Maestro...

I think the ceramics work gave me some street cred, because when I decided to paint my Beetle, I was assigned a bay in the auto shop to take care of it. And when I showed up with a couple of rolls of masking tape and newspaper for the windows and chrome, a 2.5" brush, and two quarts of Rustoleum enamel, the Maestro grinned, but didn't boot... or hoot, now I think of it... me out.

It took several sessions. I was careful to keep it neat and trim, and was pleased with the results, although it still looked pretty much like somebody had taken a brush to it to perhaps prime it for a later spraying.

It was red, and when I showed it to my upstairs neighbor she was shocked... "I thought you meant Volkswagen red, and it's Campbell's Tomato Soup red!" (Nothing judgmental, just a matter of expectations to be realigned.)

Well, yes, it was, but it was what was available in the Garden-of-Eden emporium in good ol' downtown Indian Head; and it was shiny and clean and much more apt to stand out in Beltway traffic, so as not to get run over, and that was what mattered. I had originally thought to put some black dots on it as well to make it a true Lady-Bug, but decided I'd be pressing my luck with the guys at the Hobby Shop, so quit while I was ahead.

It even looked better in our parking slot in front of our building, but not too long after it was painted we discovered another Samuels was on the way.

We bought a VW Bus and began a new adventure.

The Beetle was retired to our farm for a few years where we enjoyed driving it to the river to fish, or down to the creek on a hot day. It was a fine vehicle for times when others would have been mired in and the tractor required to pull them out. With the Beetle, four passengers could get out, each man a corner, and lift the Bug out of the quagmire.

Eventually we sent our beloved Beetle to Robert's family's farm at Virginia Beach with a for sale sign on it.

In that great land of the dune buggy, it sold for the exact same $400 we had paid for it.

What a car!

Chapter Twenty-Eight

About the same time the Beetle entered our lives...

Birthday Girl

When God gives you lemons...

Daughter Amy was a force to be reckoned with right from the get-go.

When she was just past four we lived in an apartment in Greenbelt, Maryland. She was about the smallest of the neighborhood kids, and could never get a swing to play on, but had to be content with watching and hoping for better times.

Then one fine morning she broke out in a rash and the good doctor said "chicken pox" even though she wasn't feeling badly at all.

When we were back at home we got out of the car, and w-a-a-a-y before my brain had processed this as good news, Amy ran to the playground and announced loudly "I HAVE CHICKEN POPS!"

With that one fell swoop she cleared the grounds... and for one joyous day she had ALL the swings...

And then when God gives you tomatoes...

A few months later, summer, tomatoes from the garden were in, and from infancy Amy had loved them. When she had just turned one year old I took her to the garden in her stroller and filled the bag behind her seat with glorious ripe red tomatoes... I kept picking, and when I turned back she was holding a tomato as big as her head, and was juicily working on it with all four teeth…

Anyhow… this summer of her fourth year she developed a mysterious rash just about the time the tomatoes came in, so I decided to cut back her tomato ration to see if that was the cause. I gave her sister and myself the normal portion for lunch, and Amy got just a taste, explaining that I thought maybe she was allergic to them.

You'd have thought I'd ripped her heart out.

She yelled and stormed and cried and kicked and beat her fists on the table and then yelled some more…

…and then all of a sudden the room went dead quiet.

Her sister Lisa and I looked at each other and then at Amy, and waited in the silence for the other shoe to fall.

It did.

Amy, at four years old, announced in a very solemn voice "GOD just spoke to me."

Even at age four, she had us trained right. Lisa and I said in unison "What did He say?"

"He said I was not allergic to tomatoes," she pronounced, "and I could have all I wanted."

Well, I've always liked to pick my battles, and seldom pick one with someone who has God on her side… Amy got her tomatoes, and suffered no ill effects at all…

Not too long after, we found the source of the "allergy". It was a little rabbit fur purse that was a birthday gift. She had liked it so well she held it in her hot sweaty little hands long enough and often enough to get a contact rash…

This day is a special one many years later…Happy Birthday to the Unsinkable Amy Lou! She can still clear a playground, and God still talks to her, and I'll bet He listens, too!

Chapter Twenty-Nine

To Every Thing...

A typical "spring's coming" day in Virginia... a couple of 70 degree days after bitter cold and snow, followed now by rain and winds and a rapidly dropping barometer, a low worthy of a hurricane, to be followed tomorrow by bitter cold again then 70 in a couple of days. Welcome to March, Virginia-style.

All of which means that it's time for one of my favorite things: starting seedlings for the garden.

In 1963 we received as a premium for joining a "selection of the month" Book Club three magnificent books that we could not possibly have afforded otherwise. One of them was a passing fancy, I suppose, because I have no idea what it was; but the second was a big, beautiful collection of Audubon's bird plates for Robert; and the third was Taylor's "Encyclopedia of Gardening" for me.

We were living in a tiny apartment, finishing up at Washington State University. No yard and no real prospects of one in the near future, but I have always, always loved plants and garden things.

I devoured the entire Encyclopedia, and still can see the placement of articles on a given page, and quote lots of data I've never had occasion to use. I still use that tome as reference, although it threatens to fall apart when I take it from the shelf. It's full of obscure notes and wildflowers I've gathered and pressed, flyers from herb gardens and seed catalogues. Wonderful book!

When we left WSU, after a brief stop in Virginia to have a baby Amy, and a train trip to Texas for Robert's commissioning, we headed for Massachusetts, bought the only house we could afford, and since it was November, I began planning my first garden.

I knew I couldn't afford to buy tomato and pepper plants, but I could surely eke out some seed money, so I started my lifelong relationship with the Park Seed Company. What a wonderful winter wishbook! … And since the thermometer never broke 17 degrees that first February, dreaming of Spring was never better.

I started the seeds according to Taylor's and the packet instructions, and in less than 2 weeks had a bumper crop of little tomatoes and green peppers helping me celebrate every three-minute addition to the lengthening days.

Our oldest daughter loved watching all this happen too… she also had a relationship with growing things, and loved rolling the names of plants off her three year old tongue… Thanks to her, we grew "cactopusses" and "gazinnias ", and the ranunculus bulb I was so proud of turned into a "galunculus"… this I heard for the first time when she came running in to tell me the Galunculus had a Big Orange Bloom!

Baby Amy was one year old when the our first garden tomatoes ripened, and while I was weeding and harvesting, she'd reach over into the tote on the back of her stroller and grab a tomato as big as softball, and attack it like a garden turtle, then grin with tomato juice and seeds running all the way down to her diaper top.

The garden came in spectacularly that year, and I was hooked for life.

I've added seed purveyors over the years, this year ordering from several well-stocked seed catalogues to get varieties I like. The seed and plant companies know when I've made my last wreath of the year and have "walking around money" as Robert always called it, and their catalogues arrive almost on the second… It's cold, it's dark and I'm house-bound. You know about a fool and his money… well, a gardening fool works twice as fast to stop that fire in the pocket.

I use styrofoam cups for starting seeds instead of something more environmentally sound because they give better soil temperature stability when I start moving the babies outdoors to harden them off. I punch holes in the bottoms for drainage, which can be exciting when I put the spare cups away, then forget and serve drinks in them…

(A better use for the leftover styro cups: break them up for use in pot bottoms for drainage. I never seem to have enough clay shards for this, and these Styrofoam "shards" work just fine. Makes me feel better about the eco-hostile thing, too.)

I plant one or two seeds to the cup, water a little, topdress with perlite or vermiculite to keep "damp-off" from doing in the little guys; then cover with something mostly air tight and put in any stable spot for a few days, until I peek in and see little green arms waving back at me. Then I move the babies to a bright window, or under lights, or both… take off the cover, and voila, (or Vi-ol-a, as a friend says) enjoy the miracle!

In about six-eight weeks, the plants are just right for the garden. Sometimes the garden is just right too. In other years the plants have to wait for settled weather. They like being set out late in the day on a windless, overcast day. They'll settle for two out of three.

Sometimes with tomatoes and peppers I break out the bottom of the cup to use as a collar for the young plants, to thwart the cutworms that can destroy all my work in a day.

When I was first gardening around my father-in-law, who ran a magnificent garden every year, he came in the kitchen with a sheepish look and an uprooted tomato plant in hand… He explained he'd thought I had planted the tomato in the cup, and not knowing I'd cut the bottom out, picked it up to let me know that that method wouldn't work.

Basil's great fun from seed though it can take 4-5 weeks (to the devil and back, according to herbals) to sprout. The dear friend who mentored my first herb garden, said I would know the little basils because their first pair of leaves would look like chubby little baby fists, and to this day, that's what I think of when I see them. It was this same mentor who also told me that to know the difference between an infant herb and an infant weed in the garden, just sniff… if it smells good, you just pulled up an herb.

Ordinarily I direct sow squash and Swiss chard in the garden, but the deer and squirrels have been so voracious of late that I'm going to start a couple of each indoors to put in the mini-bed by the deck, in hopes of being able to fend off the varmints. For the main garden, am going to try hot pepper wax this year in the fervent hope of hearing "A-i-e-e-e-e Caramba!" as the varmints speed away.

Yeah, I know, I'm dreaming… But that's what gardeners do.

Spring

Silver-y grey days… In the enthusiasm of early spring after one heck of a winter, the sap can rise at an alarming rate. I want to do it ALL, NOW!... and of course, that can't happen without some burn-out… aches, hay fever, or just the discontinuity of being so excited to do it all that everything gets a kiss and a promise…

Hence, silver-grey days like this one… mist in the lowgrounds, fog infusing the petals of dogwood and redbud so they stretch out as you watch, and you watch more consciously because you're not so busy DOING.

In a month the irises will be blooming. I've always felt they were made of the stuff of these silvery-grey days, coming out of the mist and melting back into it…

I'll spend today like Jack Beagle… stretched out enjoying, so I can run twice as hard next time.

Chapter Thirty

Grand Kids

When my grandchildren were just a little past "twinkle in the eye" stage, they decided I would be "Gunga". I won't lie to you— it took a little getting used to— but I can state unequivocally now that it is one of the most beautiful words in the English language…

Almost the birthday of my eldest Grandchild, now making, along with his cousins and siblings the transition from great kid to great adult. There's a reason they're called "grand" kids, y'know…

There may yet be things that are as intrinsically wonderful as grandchildren ahead, like great-grandchildren or golden slippers; but they surely won't be as much fun or as joyful to watch; and to have been accepted as a "fellow" by them has been such a gift— the one that really does keep on giving.

Note: I'm not talking grand-babies here. I like looking at them, but can't wait for them to get big enough to be interesting. Happily, other folks like the teeny ones, so it works out.

From my Florida grands I've learned that you can paint tree carts and dig French drains and bust up cement for Pampaw, and he'll buy a spinner so you can learn to shoot the .22. You can learn to use the riding lawnmower, and then learn to go slowly enough to actually let the grass know you're there.

I was privileged to give driving instruction as well as rifle instruction to two grands. No problem, I already had my grey hair. And a couple of you even learned to drive the old straight stick F150!

You did great with the kayaks, and put them back in good order, too…

You fixed your own breakfast when you were so little the firstborn had to stand on the counter to get the bowls out for the rest!

Together we raised turtles and mantises and salamanders, and caught and released lightning bugs… we built boxes and played the guitar and sang … and amazed the Christmas tree customers by running barefoot, December or no…

We all got to shoot skeet together for the first time, and I was happy to even stay in the running with you Annie and Andy Oakleys.

The four Florida Grands plus four friends arrived last year after a 14 hour trip from Florida to find the farm decimated by a "derecho" just in time for the family reunion.

No power? No problem… All the teens took the truck and headed for the river! I'm not even sure they knew the power was out. They fished and cooked on the grill, bathed and dug a latrine, kayaked and tubed… And despite it all, they were here Saturday night spit shined and fine for the Fourth, reunion time at Foxfire…

So dear grand-people, while you're transitioning, and winding up school and taking jobs and getting significant others, know that I am unbelievably proud of you all.

And I'm looking forward to your getting two-week vacations, and in time even bringing those significant others (and yes, even those "babbies"… I know they'll be interesting ones even early on)…

And I'm still enjoying every wonderful minute you were here…

And I'm eternally grateful to your good parents for you, and for their generousity in sharing their finest treasure with me.

Much love…

Gunga

Part Three

Adventures with Other-Legged Folks

Excepting the chickens, two legged, but rather differently ; Big Jim and his kith and kin, no-legged; Tom, the piling-sitter at four legs; and the blue crabs, eight legged; this anthology has featured for the most part some of my favorite two-legged folks.

If you have come this far, you are probably the sort of reader who knows that love and laughter come in many packages, so I present to you an assortment of Other-Legged Folks, not necessarily of the Human Persuasion, with whom I have had the pleasure of being along for the ride…

Chapter Thirty One

The Hawk of Foxfire

The hawk that hangs out here at the farm is my late husband Robert, who always said he was coming back as one...

He nearly always turns up flying at treetop level when anything big is going on with the Christmas trees, especially during the months of wreath and tree sales when he needs to keep an eye on the cash register. (When he was in human form, Sister Skits swore he could hear the cash register buzz on his deerstand a mile away and come running, "What did you do wrong this time??") In his hawk-form once when I had done something I was particularly pleased with on the farm, he actually gave me a fly-by and wing waggle...and I guess he was still getting used to the flying thing, because he almost flew into my windshield!

All our tree and wreath workers are convinced the hawk is Robert, too, so I wasn't surprised when our ace wreath lady Rita walked into the shop one morning and said matter-of-factly "Robert's back..."

I said "Great!"

She said "... and I hate to tell you but he's got a woman with him."

Chapter Thirty-Two

The Colonel

Cat Extraordinaire

He came to live with us in Greenbelt, Maryland in 1968, just weaned, barely as large as Robert's hand, half Siamese, all black, and full of vinegar and other liquid. We called him Colonel because we felt it in his best interest that Robert never out-rank him; and Susie, because that's what our daughters, ages 4 and 6, wanted to name him.

At that age, probably 12" inches long, of which half was tail, his favorite game was to run across the back of the sofa— that's the actual back, so he was defying gravity— then scurry up over the top and attack with tooth and claw any unsuspecting soul who happened to be seated there. (Note: the little people were exempt from this treatment, or Colonel wouldn't have lasted. However, if they had misbehaved and were being reprimanded, he would swat their ankles all the way back to their room. The "Siamese" part had to come out some way...)

At about 8 months he was spending time outside each day in our apartment complex and along with teen-age acne and a changing voice, developed a taste for the ladies.

He'd come in when we went to bed, about eleven usually, and settle in for the night. We had the basement apartment, so our bedroom window was at grass-level... just right for a serenade... and serenade is what we got.

About 3 a.m. on any given night, looking out our bedroom window put us eye to eye with what appeared to be the entire cast of "Cats", the blond and beautiful, the halt and the lame, all lovesick and yowling in wild disharmony.

This went on for about a week until the morning I woke to find Robert already in uniform, headed out for the day, w-a-a-a-y early. He grabbed the Colonel under his arms, and later said he could see lights in the back of the vet's office and knew someone was there, so kept beating on the door until the attendant came, whereupon Robert thrust the cat at him saying "Fix him. I'll pick him up this afternoon."

I didn't know until years later that Colonel had gotten lucky that day. After we came to the farm Robert and one of his hunting friends fixed the farm cats themselves. After all, they did cattle all the time, so I guess they figured it was just a matter of scale. Happily, they never lost a customer.

After that, the bevy of felines gave our boy a rest. Since I always liked to keep Colonel away from the local canines when possible, I started letting him out at 6 a.m., when it was too early for most 2- and 4- legged creatures. He'd be back in for the day by 6:30, and life was good, I thought.

From kittenhood, Colonel had invented a game, which involved my holding my arm out straight and letting him do a standing jump from the floor, landing with front and rear legs wrapped around my arm. It was quite a feat for a three pound kitten, but even more impressive when he got to be a twelve pound cat... All I had to do was stick my arm out, and boom, whaddya know, there's a 12 pound cat wrapped around it....

One fine morning I opened the sliding glass patio door and let Colonel out as usual, and left the door ajar so he could come back in at will.

Half an hour later he came ripping back in, tail as big around as he was, and hot on his heels was a local policeman in full regalia.

I asked him in, and once we established that Colonel was indeed my cat, he said that the aforesaid cat had attacked a child outside the building next door and "...the child had just stuck out her arm to pet him and the cat jumped on her arm..."

I was of course distressed. Happily, there was no damage done to the child.... I apologized profusely to the Mom, who spit out (remember, this was during the anti-military Viet Nam protest times) that that's the way military people were.

The policeman said the cat would need to be confined for two weeks even though his rabies vaccine was documented, so Colonel spent two weeks in lockdown, after which we decided that it would be in his best interest to get the hell out of Dodge, so he went to spend time in the country... at my Mom's house in Virginia Beach, where there was a pond, lots of birds and ducks, where Colonel could be a free spirit again, loving the Beach life while we found housing at Indian Head Naval Station, where he could rejoin us.

After he joined us on the base it was eventually decreed that cats had to be walked on leashes.

Colonel brought all the neighbors out to watch by pulling enough slack with his paws to keep from choking to death, and allowing me to drag him wherever I wished. (It seemed a bit discriminatory since my next door neighbor walked his boa constrictor every day, sans leash. No one mentioned this to him... don't know if it was the snake, the black belt in karate, or that he was the tri-service expert on unconventional warfare devices, but he walked his snake in peace.)

Our apartment in Indian Head had once been two apartments, but at some point the two were combined to make one huge one, six of these to a building. The combining created a l-o-o-o-n-g hall, with closets having sliding metal doors nearly the whole length.

Colonel saw this as an opportunity for self-expression, and loved to wind up tight at one end of the apartment and barrel the whole way down the hall mostly sideways, as on the sofa in earlier years, hitting each door BLAM- BLAM-BLAM- BLAM...

The downstairs neighbors said that whenever we were away on vacation that's how Colonel would amuse himself, so they knew he was all right. Great neighbors...

Over time the cat somehow managed to leave black-paw scuff marks on the doors from hitting them so regularly. Robert came in the dining room after inspecting them one day and said "You know, I don't mind that he does that… but if that S.O.B. thinks I'm paying for retreads, he's got another think coming."

One fine warm New Year's Eve we invited our beloved upstairs neighbors to help usher in the New Year. I had lit all the candles I had, which were many, in the windows, on the tables, and atop the china cabinet.

It was warm, and the steam heat pipes that ran under our floor made it downright tropical, so I left the front door slightly ajar.

We were having a delightful peaceable time when Colonel Susie decide to go on a routine tear thru the house, this time culminating in a five-and-a-half foot leap to the top of the china cabinet, where he landed directly over a lit candle.

The next five seconds passed like molasses as we watched him arch his back (raising his stomach) higher and higher, still not getting it, until he finally DID, then let out an ear-splitting yowl and went hurtling out of the house and into the night, with the USAF's finest, Captain Samuels and our dear neighbor Major Overall, in hot pursuit, tearing thru the pitch black night looking for the pitch black cat.

Thank God it was not a flaming cat, though he would no doubt have been easier to find… but the Northwest Mounties had nothing on our guys… they came home cat-in-hand, none of them much the worse for wear, though it was a while before Colonel assayed the china cabinet again.

We were still in Indian Head when we bought the farm in Buckingham, and every Friday, weather permitting, we'd load kids, cat, and supplies into our Volkswagen and head for Buckingham, where Colonel spent the happiest days of his life, unfettered by leashes and rules, surrounded by mice and rabbits and all the good things cats love.

He knew when we crossed the James River, and would ride the last 12 miles with his sweaty paws on the dash, just watching for "home".

It's a wonderful thing that he lived to be nearly twenty years old, and his last years were spent full time in Buckingham, where we buried this World Class Cat on the hill looking out over the river, the mountains, and best of all, his farm.

R.I.P. Beloved Hellraiser

Chapter Thirty-Three

Sarge and the Deck Snow

Snow in the forecast.

Battening down the hatches... lots of bird food out, moved anything on the deck that would not benefit from having the whole snowload off the long side of the roof come piling down on it...

In the Great (one of them) Snow of '96 we still had our old cat Sarge, to whom I had once administered a "Cat IQ test" of about ten activities....

Sarge flunked every one, including the empty grocery bag (he went to sleep in it) and even failed the one about putting a piece of tape on the bridge of his nose. Apparently it "didn't bother him none"...

... but he was a sweet old guy and we loved him just the same.

So it came to pass that Robert and I were standing at the glass door admiring the sunshine after the big storm and Sarge was on the deck looking up when the whole glacier of roof-snow let go... WHUMPF! and Sarge was gone.

Now this was a four-foot high deck-wide avalanche, so both of us were frantically digging with shovel, hoe and whatever else we could grab, trying desperately to find our cat, until we had exhausted both our options and ourselves....

We looked up, and guess who was watching us, safely out of danger across the deck, wearing that slightly nonplussed look he so often wore, as if to say "What the heck you idiots doing now?"

Time to don the ski pants and take Sister Skits her Never-Dark generator book, then move the bucket-Kubota where I can get to it...

Take care, World, stay warm!

Chapter Thirty-Four

A Love Song for Snappy

Sounds like a line straight out of Mickey Spillane: It's not every day that a long-legged curly-haired redhead named Gingersnap comes along and grabs your heart and makes it sing, but it happened to me, and I wouldn't have missed it for all the world.

I had lost a wonderful Chessie named Willow a year earlier, and despaired of having another of those wonderful brick-headed whiskey-eyed creatures. The going price for Chesapeake Bay retriever puppies was $800. All the same, ever hopeful, I was browsing Craig's List and there she was.

Her family, who loved her dearly, had to downsize their dog population, and since they had a best beloved older Chessie they could not bear to part with, they decided to share their 18-month old with someone offering a suitable home at a price I could afford.

Her family lived near my sister, so I asked her to go on a mission for me and visit to see whether this pup might be the one. Sister Skits soon emailed back "She's beautiful! Photos attached.". And so she was.

Margaret, my Georgia cousin and loving owner of several "best-beloved" dogs, knew how much I had missed Willow, and insisted on treating me to this new puppy. Then one good neighbor built a worthy doghouse, and another put up a fine big pen, since Gingersnap, or Snappy as we began to call her, was accustomed to the "kennel up" command for nights and rainy days.

Gingersnap was a community project right from the get-go.

A couple of weeks later we went to pick her up.

I think her only real experience with car travel had probably been for puppy shots, so she was less than impressed with the idea of getting in the car. It took her Mom, my sister and I all three to get 85 pounds of determined puppy into the car and safely close the lift gate, so once she was loaded we traveled pretty much nonstop to her new farm where I opened the door and said "Welcome to Foxfire!"

She looked me in the eye and said "That's all well and good, and I'm sure you're a fine person, but this is not home and I'm not getting out, and you can pull my head off with that leash if you want, but all it'll get you is a headless dog in your car."

There were times in my life when I might have been hassled by this, but age is good for a few things, and so I waited, chatting with her, and offering a bucket of fresh water and treats. After an hour or so the farm began to look less foreign and more interesting, and out she came.

Of course I knew there would soon come a time when she would need to be a willing traveler, since shots and spaying were in her near future, so after a day or two of letting her get used to her new home, I put her leash on and opened the car gate and said, in my most positive and cheerful voice, "Okay, Snap, hop in!"

She gave me the same look and message she had earlier about getting *out* of the car. I tugged on her leash and encouraged her until I was worried she was going to look like a giraffe with her neck all stretched out…

I finally managed to shove her in, but of course, when I let go to close the lift gate, she slithered right out again, sat nicely, and said quietly, "Told you so."

It was time for me to fall back and regroup. Chesapeake Bay retrievers are noted for looking people right in the eye, and studying them at length, and are really good at staying one step ahead of their "masters". I would need to be both wise and wily.

That evening I cooked a nice little venison roast, and when it was cool, sliced it into delectable treat-sized pieces, wrapped and froze many of them, but saved out several days' worth. In the morning I put Snappy's leash on her and we went to the van and opened the lift gate.

I held on to the leash and, assuming my role as leader of our "pack", crawled in, (not to get much into age issues, but crawling around in a van is not what it once was for me) with Snap watching me attentively from her seat on the grass. I talked a while, then opened the venison treats and let her get a good whiff, and then a taste.

I moved the treat hand further back in the van, but was still sitting there, and after some thought she hopped in beside me, got her treat and immediately turned to get out, but I managed to close the lift gate with both of us inside, then I crawled over the passenger bench seat and into the driver's seat and we drove to... here comes the wily part... the Creek!

If you know about Chesapeake Bay retrievers, you know that water is where they'd *always* rather be; and Snappy was a happy camper.

I had bought a Frisbee for the occasion, and threw it up the creek for her over and again. She would bring it back and drop it for me most of the time, but really loved burying it in the mud on the creek bank, then using her huge paws to muck it out.

By the time I was ready to go, Snap and the bank looked like a hog and her wallow, and the shiny new Frisbee looked like a strangely fringed 4" disk, but she'd had a wonderful car trip!

Until the venison treats ran out she kept me believing she needed them to get in the car; and I became fairly adept at crawling over one seat and between the others; but when the day came the treats were gone and the choice was Be Stubborn, or Miss the Creek, the Creek won.

Not too long after that I took her to the river, which she enjoyed, but she always loved the creek best, exploring it upstream and down, while I sat on the back deck of the van watching her or reading, with NPR playing loud enough to keep the bears away. (We have bears here now, but I am convinced that no self-respecting bear would be caught dead listening to NPR. So far, so good)

Snappy Moves In

Gingersnap had never experienced indoor living, and the general consensus seemed to be that she would not make a good indoor pet, nor would she ever be house trained. As I mentioned, good neighbors had built her a big pen and a wonderful doghouse and she very quickly made these her home turf, and spent lots of time in the pen the first week or so, until I felt she had her bearings and wouldn't get lost running a deer.

I did miss having a dog in the house though, not necessarily at night, but from time to time during the day when the weather was lousy or I couldn't be outside much, so I kept inviting her in.

At first Snappy's take on coming in the house was just like first getting in the van, i.e., "not gonna happen"; but by now she and the venerable black cat Bill had reached détente, and she could see thru the glass door that good things, like FOOD, happened to Bill in the house, so she decided to chance it; and it was ALL good!

There was a comfortable dog bed, and things always falling on the floor at sandwich making time. There was even a naptime, and naps are another Chessie specialty (Chessies have a wonderful purring kind of snore). The kennel still worked fine for night time, but the house was not so bad after all.

The upstairs was a still a mystery though. She would watch me climb the stairs, then listen to my footsteps and follow them through all the downstairs rooms, then come back to sit at the foot of the stairs, head cocked, trying to puzzle it all out.

One afternoon when I had been upstairs at the computer longer than usual, I felt eyeballs on me. I looked around from the computer to see Snap peeping around the office door. As soon as we made eye contact, she was gone like the wind, breakneck back down to the bottom of the stairs.

Of course, after that she got a little bolder, then a little braver, and when she finally began to explore upstairs and found she could see *forever* out the windows (and not only that there was a comfortable bed upstairs too!), she became a regular upstairs companion whowould join me in the evening to watch a little TV.

She was fascinated by and very curious about the dogs and cats in commercials, and left lots of large noseprints on the otherwise pristine flatscreen. One of my daughters had taken a look at our first Chessie and said "Her nose looks just like a mucilage bottle." I found it functioned much the same, especially on flatscreens and glass doors.

I had gotten in the habit of putting her out at eight o'clock, but after a week or so, didn't have to call her. As soon as she heard the final theme music from Jeopardy, she'd be at the door waiting to go. We'd go outside, I'd say "Kennel up!" and she'd go right in to bed. Of course, once she could stay in the house with no housetraining disasters, she inveigled herself in for the night, too.

Snappy's Pack

When I had decided to get a dog, I'd begun reading about the care and raising of them for the first time (after a lifetime of having dogs around!) and was interested in the meaning of the pack to a dog, and how a dog looks for leadership to the senior and wisest of the pack, which works out well if he/she happens to be the owner.

Snappy, raised with an older Chessie, never had any desire to be the chief dog, and seemed to be perfectly happy letting me be the leader, and Bill-the-Cat second in command. (We didn't burden Bill with this information. Everybody knows cats aren't second in command to anyone. Bill would have been traumatized.)

Snap woke up every morning ready to run out and seize the day, and Bill took a more leisurely approach, studying the great outdoors to see 1. whether it was safe and 2. whether there was anything out there that was worthy of the morning's hunt.

Snap, meantime, would have made several circuits of the yard, and remembering her pack etiquette, be back at the door, tongue down to her knees, saying "C'mon, Bill, c'mon! It's a great day to be leader of our pack!" ... and Bill would mosey out as only a cat can mosey, body English clear to everybody but Snap that "Yeah, yeah, I'm coming, but

I'm a solo act, Buck-o, not the leader of anybody's pack", and together they'd set off on the day's adventure.

I do think Bill was privately delighted in having a 100 pound sidekick; and the two of them enjoyed napping on the rug together after the hunt. Whenever Snappy had been out alone, as soon as she'd lie down, Bill would do a foot check, sniffing each of her feet to find out where she had been and whether she did anything interesting while there.

Snap Meets the Neighbors

Gingersnap's first intro to the neighborhood was to the good soul who built her new house, our farm manager Chris. They hit it off right away, and Snappy soon found that Chris came with a lot of nice extras: his wife, a real pushover for a puppy; a 4-year old son and his brand new sister; and their dog, Kayla. Kayla has a very impressive bark, just so you know she *is* a chief dog, although if she's called on it, she shrugs and says "Or whatever".

We wondered if Snappy would be too big and bouncy for the four-year old, but their first time playing together answered that. It was during one of those wonderful summer evening rains that linger in everybody's childhood memory, and he and Snap were chasing 'round and 'round, and with every round, little fellow's britches were getting soggier and soggier and dragging lower and lower, till he came out of them entirely… and neither he nor Snap had missed a step. They both slept very well that night.

Most evenings Snappy and I would walk up to the next farm, which was mostly the property of a border collie named Millie; and part-time, a beagle named Charlie Brown. On our arrival, each dog would get a treat. Snappy's and Charlie Brown's, of course, were gone almost before they knew they had them, but Mil liked to take hers back to her pen to eat at her leisure.

Just as the Creek was Snap's idea of Heaven, Millie most favorite thing was to hop in the farm truck and ride around inspecting her cattle. Given any options, she would have chosen being in the truck, whether it was going anywhere or not. She was in her favorite company, and running the place without the actual having to run part.

She was also very much a chief dog, and many's the young whippersnapper who thought that forty pound ball of black and white fur was a pushover. Millie straightened them all out, the large and the small alike, so that the next time they encountered Mil, they were more inclined to salute and say "Sir".

Snappy recognized this pretty quickly, and would sit respectfully on the opposite side of the lane when Mil was out. (Sometimes, if Charlie Brown was around, he and Snap would sit together across the road and mutter a few less than praiseful remarks about the top sergeant across the way.)

There were some advantages to being on that side of the road, though… that's where the occasional baseball game happened, and the first time Snappy saw all that action going on she sat and studied it for a long time, knowing that a dog must fit in there somewhere, but not quite sure where to jump in.

Her moment came when a grounder came rolling right to her. She snagged it, started to run away with it, but without too much persuasion put it back in play.

The kids were kind, and let her stay in the game; and nobody mentioned that the new player had turned a perfectly good baseball game into a game of slobberball.

Sometimes on visits to Millie's house Mil was in her kennel, and Snap could visit with Mil's owner, getting lots of head and ear scratching in the process, which was just fine.

Mil's owner has amazing rapport with animals great and small, and he soon introduced Snappy to one of the reasons for his uncanny puppy-rapport: Hot Dogs! He kept a pack of Hot Dogs in the barn fridge just for his four legged friends! What a Prince of a man!

Snap's attitude adjustment at this new information was fun to watch. Where before Mil's master had been a nice guy who'd scratch your ears for you if you happened to wander by, now she would sit at his knee, gazing up with absolutely adoring eyes, and I swear, she somehow made her ears and eyelashes longer and curlier… and if he didn't notice soon enough that she was telling him something, she'd leave his side just long enough to gently bump the door to the fridge room where the hot dog stash was kept.

Shameless!

Gingersnap Rides Shotgun

By September the ride-shy puppy was a seasoned traveler who would hop into the van at a moment's notice. She had discovered Road Rabbits* on our walks, and would run like the wind with those long legs stretching out, chasing them for all she was worth.

When the weather cooled, we began taking a ride in the evening around the large circle that is our neighborhood, checking to be sure everything was safe and in its appointed place. She'd stand in the back of the van with her elbows resting on the back of the passenger seat, eyes on the road ahead until I said "Road Rabbit", then she'd lurch around the van following the little critter from every window in the vehicle.

When we added "Squoil" to her vocabulary we had enough game options to keep the van rocking with 100 pounds of Chessie careening around the van interior like Evel Knievel in the motorcycle cage.

*Road Rabbits are the ones you always see in the middle of gravel roads. My husband told his little Cub Scout passengers one evening that they shouldn't shoot Road Rabbits. When one of the little guys asked why not he told them "It's dangerous. You can't eat them because they're full of gravel, and when you shoot them the shot ricochets all over the place and might kill you." Wide-eyed, they believed him.

Gingersnap goes to Work

Our farm is a choose-and-cut Christmas tree plantation, and Thanksgiving, when we opened for business, was Snappy's debut as Foxfire's Christmas Tree Dog.

Kayla was also around the shop during the season, having a wonderful time being more-or-less chief dog, and one of the best visuals I have in memory of shop season is the day I parked the van at the shop with the back gate up, getting ready to put a load of freshly made wreaths on for town delivery later in the day.

Kayla saw the gate open and jumped in, and went up to sit behind the wheel in the driver's seat, and was enjoying the view from there. Snappy noticed this, and put two and two together… the chief dog was getting ready to drive somewhere!

Not to miss a good ride, Snap hopped in the back and put her elbows up on the passenger seat; and when I saw them, Kayla in the driver's seat and Snap eager to go right behind her, I knew Snap was saying "Okay, Kayla, let's hit the road!"

Gingersnap, Christmas Tree Dog

Our earlier Chessies had done a wonderful job of being Christmas Tree dogs during their twenty-five years, and we had every reason to think Snappy would also; at the same time, that's a lot of strangers to meet and greet with a wag of the tail, and a lot of little folks to be gentle with, especially for a bouncy 2-year old pup.

Not to worry.

She quickly discovered that toddlers with candy cane all over their faces were the most fun for puppy kisses; and that customers really appreciated it if the Foxfire Dog went with them to find THE tree.

The second week she hosted tree-cutting she got fan mail, a first for any of the Tree Dogs of Foxfire.

Foxfire has several fine wreath-making Elves, and all of them are pushovers for a good dog, particularly Rita.

Rita could always be counted on for a kind word or a good ear-scratching, most often accompanied by a treat of some kind; and a couple of times Rita brought her good dog Joey over to play. He and Snap had a wonderful time running as hard and fast as they could.

Snap slept hard and snored loud as a freight train after her "Joey" playdates.

Snap and the Group Hug

Snappy's life was complicated by the fact of having a mixed two- and four-legged pack. I believe she used that long thoughtful gaze of hers to decide which traits to adopt from each subset.

Most of her habits, of course, were of the 4-legged sort; but there was one 2-legged custom she deemed worthy.

Snap always was especially fond of sister Skits; after all, Skits was the first member she'd met of her new "pack". She had noticed that every time Skits came to visit for a few days, I would go out with greetings and salutations and, of course, a big hug.

Imagine Skits' and my surprise when she arrived for one weekend, stepped out of the car, and I gave her the ritual big hug... and Snappy stood up on her hind legs, making her taller than either of us, put an arm around each of our shoulders, and made it a Group Hug, tail wagging and tongue delivering puppy kisses all the while.

The Hug was mostly reserved for Skits and I, though she tried it once with someone else who was not entirely sure about big dogs who kept all four feet on the ground, let alone six foot tall Hugging Dogs.

Snap sensed her reservations, and after that kept her hugs for Skits and I until the day she perceived a Very Great Need for one of her special embraces.

A Christmas Hug

One of our dearest Christmas Tree Families, a young husband and wife with small children, had one of those times several years back that tests body and spirit.

The doctors had located several tumors in the husband's brain. They were inoperable, and when they came to cut their Christmas tree my conversation with the young wife made clear that the prognosis was not good.

The whole family had a wonderful time getting their tree and the children had loved running and playing with Snappy's predecessor, Willow.

In the spring that year Willow passed away after a long and happy life. A few weeks after, I decided to call the family to see how things were going, and there was very good news… the tumors had gone away!

We had a good conversation, catching up, and I mentioned that we had lost Willow.

The wife and mother thanked me for letting her know, so she could tell the children before they came for a tree next time.

"You know, Mrs. Samuels, we talk about Foxfire and Willow all year long, and when the children are bored, sometimes we play a game that starts with '…and what do you think Willow is doing at Foxfire today?', and the children makeup stories about what adventures she might be having." I was so glad I'd called.

This last December the dear folks came in and met Gingersnap and loved her instantly, and she ran with the children till none could run any more.

While the children were running I had a chance to see how things were going with their folks, and it had indeed been a very rough year. The tumors were back and had spread, and radiation and chemotherapy lay ahead. Thankfully, the pain was controlled, but the strain was visible in Mama and Papa, each of whom confided in me about feeling that the other one had the tougher job. The future seemed once again very uncertain for all.

When all the running was done and it was time to leave, I put my arms around these two remarkable human beings in the hope they would be well and happy when we should see each other again... and Snappy, somehow perceiving the need, stood up and put her long fuzzy arms around all of us!

Snap was still a lot of puppy... but inside was a very old soul.

Sad News

In the spring of this year, on Easter Sunday, good dog Millie left us; and less than two weeks later, Gingersnap was gone as well.

Four wheels trumps four paws, every time.

Look Up

As a child I had no problems believing in the magical, mystical or miraculous. I came from a clan that never placed artificial fences in the possibilities of the Universe. So I am sure that the life force that was Snappy and the life force that was Mil are out there somewhere, shaping the future.

A few years back, our regional Governors' School students were assigned the task of using their richly inventive minds to name new heavenly constellations, and then create the mythology to go with them. I had an opportunity to read about several of these astronomical wonders, and they were wonderful...

So I intend to lie in the grass in July when the Milky Way is a great shimmering sash across the sky, and I expect to see a new constellation.

It will roughly resemble a pickup truck, with a smallish canine shape on the driver's side, and a largish one, with lots of variable stars constantly moving, on the passenger side. If I look closely at the smaller figure, I'm sure I'll see a star in the muzzle area flash sharply from time to time, when Canis Mil barks to Canis Gingersnap "... and stop schmutzing the windshield looking for Road Rabbits already!"

Bon aventure, my friends...

Elizabeth Samuels   2010

Chapter Thirty-Five

Carson's Cat

When Carson came to help out at Foxfire he came with a pair of remarkable and obviously well-loved four-footed friends.

We met his wonderful old blue-tick hound, Jill, when she came to work with Carson at the Wreath Factory. Jill had a fine hound-dog voice that any choir director would envy. If you know the folk song "Old Blue", be assured in your heart the song could as easily have been written about Jill. She was that special kind of a girl…

(If you don't know the song, you've missed a treat. Joan Baez and The Byrds, among others, recorded it, but I think Cisco Houston did it best)

Jill had some age on her, and sadly, passed away early this year, but as the song says, we know she's "… gone where all the Good Dogs go…", and I'm certain she's "…treeing possum's in Noah's Ark…"

Carson's other four footed friend is a peaceable gentleman of a cat named Swampuss (because he rose from the swamp, I'm told).

Swampy, or Swamps, as his friends call him, moves with all the grace and assurance of the man who has it all. He's a very handsome fellow with beautiful eyes; well-muscled, as a good hunter should be, but with the slightly portly physique of a man of means.

He also has a tail that some might call negligible, but I don't think they'd say that to his face. At about two inches long, it seems perfectly suited to him, nicely rounding out the whole package. I think if some tasteless soul did mention the tail thing to Swamp, he would regard that comment as that rude Jerk's problem, not his.

The Swamp-Man is unfailingly agreeable and a ready player in whatever's going on, whether it's being the Shop Cat at the Wreath Factory, where you'd have sworn he'd lived all his life, to being a full blown Farm Cat hunting the woods and fields.

He and his hound dog Jill had a wonderful friendship (Carson says Jill let a young Swampy ride around on her back). This worked out well for Jack Beagle, who lives in a constant state of mutual terror and respect with his own cat, Lexie, who has been known to knock the bejaysus out of Jack from time to time just for fun.

Lexie is a smallish cat and lived her first few years at the SPCA, life on the defensive; and Swamps, as I said, has the self-assurance of the man who knows exactly who he is and doesn't need to knock anyone around to prove it... *

At any rate, the first time Swampy went up to Jack for a friendly cat "chin-marking" session, Jack sucked in his breath and stood stock still, cold sweat running off his brow, waiting for the dread CLAWS... They never came out, and he and Swamps are now quite content to pass the time of day in each other's company. (Tho' there is still a Mexican stand-off when it comes to Jack's food.)

*In fairness to Lexie, Jack has been spotted several times using her as a practice rabbit, chasing her at full speed across the yard, chomping at cat tailfeathers all the way.

Swampy has his own food dish down in the garage for visits (he and Lexie time-share the house when they're both here, one in the house, and one in the garage).

Neither Carson nor I got the "hungry" memo from the Swamp-man one busy day, and I went in the garage to find that the cat, 'way past ready for a little nosh, had very efficiently sliced open a brand-new 18 lb. cat food bag, just wide enough to accommodate his head and shoulders, building himself a sort of SuperDish for free feeding. Having taken what nourishment he needed, he was sleeping the sleep of the innocent on top of the nice warm clothes dryer.

His next experience fending for himself came a week or so later and was a little more exciting and less productive…

Once again, we humans failed to get the memo. The lid was tight on the cat food bin, so Swamp decided that dog food would do in a pinch.

Unfortunately for him, Jack's food is kept in one of those deceptively innocent looking (to a cat leaping from floor level) trash bins with a swinging lid… great for letting the food aroma out, not so great for jumping up on to get a little snack.

It must have been one heck of a ride, because the lid of the bin and a shower of dog food were strewn halfway across the mud room floor.

I'm really sorry I missed it, though I'd probably have had to laugh out loud, and that's never a good thing to do with a cat…

Swamps never com-plained or ex-plained, taking it all in with his "win some, lose some," nonchalance. Nothing gained, nothing lost… except perhaps a little dignity… and since there were no humans around, he didn't have to do what cats always do when there are observers: look cool and say "I meant to do that".

It didn't take long to figure out that the big Swamp Cat LOVES to travel, so it's important to check vehicles leaving the farm to be certain he hasn't followed his adventurous heart and jumped into a passing car, just to see what's going on a little further down the road.

I do believe he'd be perfectly content on a cross-country trip, foraging for meals and camping out under the stars. He probably has a small cat-guitar stashed somewhere for that eventuality, so he can serenade the dogies by starlight. I can see him now in my mind's eye, giving a whole new meaning to the phrase "cat-herder"…

I took advantage of his love of travel one afternoon when I was giving Carson a ride home. Carson had left, walking with Jack, and Swamps and I were to pick up the two of them down the road a bit.

Got in the car to leave, and there was no Swampy to be found. I hunted a while, and called… still no Swampy. Finally decided to see what would happen if I pressed the garage door opener.

When the Travelling Tom heard that Call of the Open Road he came flying from down by the barn… "HEY! WAIT FOR ME!"! … and leapt straightaway into the car, perching high on the seat back so as not to miss any part of whatever adventure might be ahead.

He is indeed a rambling man…

But more than travel, more than hunting, more even than sleeping atop a warm dryer, what Swampy loves most of all doing is riding around on Carson's shoulders, and I think that's my favorite visual when it comes to him.

When he is proudly taking in the world from far up in the air on the shoulders of his lanky master, he is, for the time, transformed into General Swamps, Sci-Fi Battlefield Commander, riding high atop his war machine…. A battle bot straight out of the movies…

And he's totally believable…

Fireworks

*Daylily blooms… Butterfly Weed
Shred the green brocade of Summer.*

Chapter Thirty-Six

Autobiographical Notes

My name is Jack Beagle. I'm the son of rabbit dogs Rebel and Peach, both now deceased, and to their credit, I am both a rebel and a peach.

I was one in a litter of nine, and spent my babyhood at the home of Foxfire's eastern neighbors, and I still have a special place in my heart for these folks. Every time my human Mom and I drive past their house she says "Heads up, Jack… there's your ancestral home!"

I still go over there to run when I hear the old gang of cousins singing… there's Girl and Mario and Squeaky and whoever else is around. Mom thought Squeaky was kind of a strange name for a pup until she heard him chasing a rabbit... there's no mistaking which voice is his!

I also have a baby sister over on the Big Hill... she's one of the lemon-colored beagles and they call her Lemonade (L for short!). We get together sometimes with Chase and Maggie May, who looks like kin but isn't, and spend a day de-rabbiting the west end of the neighborhood.

For those of you who haven't experienced it, hanging out with a whole pile of beagles, tails up in the air wagging, everybody singing his own song at the top of his lungs... it's the purest kind of joy!

Being a Beagle is a lot of work. Those little pink paw pads I came with are tough enough now to open cans. For my size, I'm the equivalent of a Caterpillar Earth mover; and I never, ever quit.

Once I've decided to dig something out I keep at it, yes, "dogged-ly", sometimes going back the next day to finish the job. I'm a pretty good mole-hound, too, even though rabbits are my specialty.

I've developed a route for my travels over the past 5 years, and it's led me to some fine acquaintances. I used to stop past the mailbox at Mikey's first thing... sometimes if he wasn't paying attention I could sneak a little kibble. He and I would catch up on all the local news before I set out on my rounds.

Sometimes his Mom would bring him to my house when she visited, so when a thunderstorm came up and Mike's Mom wasn't home he'd come knocking at our door looking for his Mom and/or shelter... He really didn't like storms, and I've gotten so I feel the same way about them.

A couple of years ago a big storm came up suddenly, and my Mom and I were a few inches from the glass door looking out at the rain pouring down when all of a sudden KERACK! a lightning bolt hit the big oak tree about eight feet away...

It was like a slow motion movie, crackling up the tree and blowing wood out everywhere and swirling around inside the bird feeder that hung in the tree before it blew the bejaysus out of THAT.

Neither one of us was quite right for a couple of days after, and since then I avoid storms whenever possible, usually sitting very close to Mom—to protect her of course!

Beagle Song

*Happiness is running at dusk in the cool air, a
little moonlight, rabbits everywhere,
with kinbeagles Squeaky, Girl, Mario and Rebel...
singing a capella,
listening to the 15 baby nephew and niece beagles
in the kennel practicing for their future,
all of us celebrating June.
It doesn't get any better than this...*

Chapter Thirty-Seven

Collusion: It's an Amazing Thing...

Our little lady feline, Lexie-da-Cat, has spent endless busy hours ripping a Lexie-sized hole in the corner of the screen door.

I have patched it innumerable times, and shortly after will hear her pick, pick, picking away at the corner to open it again, and when she's got it, looks at Jack and at me as if to say "Idiots!", and steps out as though magically walking through a wall.

Now Lex is a cat's cat, and always acts as though she'd be perfectly happy if Jack Beagle dropped head first off the face of the earth; but after he had spent four days on lockdown while healing from minor surgery, her heart grew four sizes, and I noticed her pick-picking again, until Jack, Joe Cool himself, was at last able to look back at me, say "Idiot", and ghost-like, step right thru the door....

Free at last!

Was it altruism or collusion? Or just that Lexie wanted dibs on prime sleeping cushions in the house?

Inquiring minds want to know...

Chapter Thirty-Eight

Things That Go WHUMP in the Night

Jack was only three months old or so, still a tiny little guy, sleeping in my rather tall bed with me when I was awakened by a very small WHUMP followed by such pitiful yelping and howling I was sure my puppy had broken every bone in his body.

I leaped out of bed and couldn't see him anywhere, and he was dead quiet, so I was fearing the worst when here he came, face poking out from under the bed, wearing the lacy dust ruffle like a bridal veil.

I told Sister Skits about his mishap the next morning, and the very next day FedEx brought him his puppy steps to use for clambering in and out of bed.

Seven years and 27 pounds later, in the middle of the night, I still hear him trudging up his steps to bed.

That gift was extremely well received, but about the same time we were in Christmas Tree season and Jack's Aunt Skits decided he needed something to keep him warm out there with the customers. To that end, she knitted him a beautiful little red sweater.

Excited for his debut into the world of fashion, we put the sweater on him.

He fell over on his side as though he'd been shot. Not only that, but he was immobilized by his new duds. He couldn't move or get up.

I don't know what he was thinking... perhaps that he was in the clutches of some dog-eating monster and had better not move...

We took it off and he was healed immediately.

One morning six years later, Jack Beagle was again asleep on the edge of the bed. When I was ready to get up I reached over to pat him...

He rolled over for a belly rub and... WHUMP!

Thank goodness, only his dignity was injured, and for someone who dumpster dives after dinner every night there's not a whole lot of dignity to injure. If there was any pain remaining, it was instantly healed when our friend Tank showed up with a sausage biscuit for him for breakfast.

Chapter Thirty-Nine

Trauma

To friends of the resident beagle:

Jack Beagle is having surgery tomorrow to remove a small growth on his hard working right front leg.... He asks for your most positive thoughts for the surgery and most especially for the *fasting... for nearly twenty-four hours!!!*

Jack: "To ensure that I don't expire from hunger between now and tomorrow p.m., I've eaten everything I could find all day long to prepare for my ordeal by starvation. I worry that I might just wizen up and blow away without access to food 24/7...."

Later:

Update on Jack Beagle: the surgery went well, Jack is home, albeit groggy. They sent the tissue to the state lab just to be on the safe side. The folks at the vet's clinic are all aces in my book....

Now the fun begins.

Jack, who runs 8-10 hours a day every day, is confined to quarters for two weeks, with no running, jumping, or stair climbing.

I disassembled a living room chair and put its fat cushion down on the floor with his favorite velvet pillow on it, sat beside it and explained how comfortable he'd be on it. He gave it and me the Beagle "in-your-dreams" look, and jumped up on the sofa. About an hour later he remembered something important he had to do upstairs, and blew right through the baby gate.

It's gonna be an exciting two weeks!

Bones, Hot Cross Buns, and Wasabi
Had an eye appointment this afternoon.

I was feeling truly compassionate for Jack Beagle in week two of being confined to quarters because of his surgery, so on the way out of town I stopped in Foods of All Nations, where they sell not only the world's finest wreaths (ours), but also wonderful dog bones cut to your dog's specs.

I picked him up six nice ones, and since it's a hard place to leave without finding other goodies, found hot cross buns for Sister Skits, and from the beautiful sushi bar, some spicy yellowfin for my supper....

Jack was delighted with his bone-du-jour and straightaway ran out to the end of his rope to bury it so he could get back in time to find out what else I'd brought to eat.

It was such a lovely evening I took my sushi and lemonade out on the deck, and of course, Jack joined me, waiting for anything that might fall on the floor and be legally his.

I decided after the first few pieces that I could probably spare a half a sushi, sans wasabi, so put it on the deck for him....

What a look!

"Do we really *eat this?* I mean, *really*???"

He finally decided since I was continuing to stuff them down they must be ok, but I don't think sushi's ever going to top his list of delectables....

In the meantime I was marveling that I had managed to put away six of the little jewels with wasabi without putting my sinuses into orbit, when the seventh one reached out and

burned...... me...... up!!!

Boy, was it good.

Chapter Forty

Jack Beagle is Churched

My name is Jack Beagle. I am a licensed rabbit hunter. It's what I do.

Along with six hours of rabbit-hunting daily, I also have a very full social calendar. I am somewhat short and small, and find that my life is much less anxiety-laden if I visit all the neighbors, and, of course, their large dogs, at least once a week, just so we're all clear that I only come in peace, folks... just here for the bunnies. (Of course if an occasional snack is proffered, just so much better. Eating is what I do second best.)

It was in the course of making my rounds last Sunday, while I was enjoying some of my favorite kids and just about ready to head home for a nosh and a nap (what I do third best), when I saw my Car go by.

The Car usually stops for me in case I want a ride, and since I was a pretty good piece away from home, that seemed like a fine idea, but this time it wasn't stopping... in fact, it wasn't even headed in the right direction!

Thinking either there was some mistake or that my Person was trying to sneak away for the day, as sometimes happens, I decided to catch up with my ride, so I started running, picking 'em up and putting 'em down as only a rabbit hound can, ears and tail strung out in the wind.

Jackson's Person:

I thought Jack was off hunting and I knew I was late for church. It was Palm Sunday and I had palms for my own church as well as for a neighboring congregation.

I was making pretty good time headed down the road when I caught a glimpse out of the corner of my eye of a familiar character, so slowed a little to double check, and sure enough, there was the Mighty Rabbit Hunter visiting some neighbor children.

Immediately I resumed speed, but too late... he'd spotted me.

I knew from past experience that outrunning him was not going to happen. A rabbit-hunting beagle is like a Northwest Mountie... he will get his man; and if he has to run for forty days and forty miles to do it, well, that's just part of the job. Happily, I had a leash in the car, so I stopped and Jackson hopped in.

Time to revisit my plans for the day. I have noticed one happy fact about getting older: when I was younger, my body was pretty flexible but my mind, not so much... nowadays, though the body is sometimes stiff as a board, the mind has learned to lighten up and bend a bit; so I felt the day was going to work out anyway despite any changes in plans.

I decided there was no time to take Jack home since I was already late, so I'd take him with me, drop off the neighbors palms and those for my church, along with the copies I'd made of the next few months' schedule of services, and head back home.

I was sorry to have to leave since it was a very special Sunday, and as our minister pointed out, we Episcopalians are not noted for reliably getting back for the rest of the Holy Week services, preferring to get most everything in one large dose on Palm Sunday; but I'd be sure to be back next Sunday for Easter.

Jack:

I thought we were going to the dumpsters. That's the only destination I've visited regularly by auto, and I love the wonderful aromas there. The history of a whole week's activities is written in redolence around those dumpsters, so I'm always happy to go…

But our vehicle wasn't the usual fragrant garden of delights that trip entails, and surely if it were trip-to-the-vet day, I'd have been on board from the start.

Curious…

We hadn't been off our gravel road long before we made our first stop.

I was wearing my best Sunday-go-to-meeting Episcopal leash, a gift from my doting Aunt Skits (the same Aunt who overnighted me a set of stairs to use getting in and out of bed after I fell off the bed and almost killed myself), so I felt suitably dressed for visiting.

We took the fine new ramp up to the doors of our sister church, and went into the vestibule. A nice lady greeted us and I remembered her from her annual visit to our farm for a Christmas tree. I think she was just as surprised to see me at the church as I was to see her, but she took it in stride and thanked us profusely for the palms.

As gracious as she was, she did look a bit relieved when we didn't head into the big room they call the Sanctuary. Instead we resumed our road trip, arriving in short order at Emmanuel Church.

We walked around outside for a few minutes, which gave me an opportunity to leave a few markers in case I ever needed to find my way back, and to let other four-legged folks know I'd visited, always a courteous thing to do. Then we went into the room called the Parish Hall to drop off the palms and the schedules.

Well, you'd have thought I was a long-lost cousin, home at last!

So many nice people I'd never met came up to scratch my ears and tell me what a fine pup I was and how nice it was to meet me. I loved it, and thanked them all with many wags.

Then came a fine surprise… the person who belongs to my absolute best bud, Joey, came in. Her name is Rita, and she's wonderful. I was so happy to see her she got lots of extra wags!

Jack's Person:

It was good to see everyone. We are a very small church, so don't have service every Sunday, and it's always nice to get together. I knew Jack would be delighted to see Rita, who with her Australian shepherd Joey had mentored him through the chew-everything-ask-later stage of puppyhood. She always had a treat in her pocket for good dogs, and was a dead-eye with a water gun when the situation demanded it….

After chatting a bit, catching up with everyone, I thought I had better go ahead and take my hound dog back to the farm. I said as much, and was headed out when our minister said "He's welcome to stay, you know."

I had no idea how Jackson Beagle would behave for an hour of quiet attentiveness. That's not generally his long suit.

I hesitated, running through possible scenarios, knowing that just because I loved Jack in all his puppyhood didn't mean other folks necessarily would… but all the folks gathered said please to stay, so I decided to sit at the back where I could leave at a moment's notice.

Rita said "I'll sit back there with you and help", so Jack and I sat on one side of the aisle with Rita across from us, and we braced ourselves for whatever lay ahead.

Jack:

We went all the way to the back of the Sanctuary. There was a door there, and I could smell the outdoors, so I knew I was all right, but there were two contraptions at the back of the room that were noisily throwing off enough heat to fry a beagle.

I didn't trust them a bit, though I guess they felt good to people at the front of the room on a chilly morning. I was just settling in when the nice Lady who said I was Welcome to stay said we should all come to the front and get our palms and walk around the church singing, so off we went.

When the music started my Person and I fell in right behind a nice man named Ned who was wearing an Angel Suit and carrying the Cross, and we paraded around and around the room with everyone singing at the top of his lungs

It didn't take me too long to figure out this exercise. A couple of times last winter I was allowed (after inviting myself) to go hunting with a pack of rabbit beagles and it was just like this… everybody going around in circles and singing in full voice. … so I knew I was in good company.

However, after about the fourth time around the same circle (me dodging those two red hot contraptions every pass) nobody had kicked up the first rabbit, so I decided to sit out the rest of the run. Maybe they'd have better luck another time.

Eventually they all figured out the same thing and sat down too.

I think I have mentioned earlier that I'm a little height challenged— too short on one end, one might say; good for putting your nose to the ground all day, not so great for hunting giraffes or seeing the front of a room from the very back.

Since I couldn't really see what was going on at all I stretched out on the red carpet with my nose pressed against the crack at the outside door, breathing in the fresh air.

My Person had already told me not to mistake the red carpet for grass, and she whispered it pretty urgently, so while I didn't get the exact wording, I got the full meaning… "Don't even think about marking this." I only thought about it once and we stepped outside for a minute where we took care of every puppy's obligation to fellow travelers.

Back inside, it was still frustrating not to be able to see what was going on at the front of the room so I jumped up on the seat to check things out. It was waxed as slick as glass and I very nearly busted my bum! But I stayed up there long enough to recover my composure.

Then I saw a wonderful sight, a gentleman approaching with a Plate! I watched patiently as he got closer and closer, and finally he was right beside me. He scratched my ears and told me what a fine dog I was… then *took the Plate to the next person without offering me a thing!*

Such nice people, I could hardly believe it had happened. When the Plate was all the way at the front of the room again the Welcome Lady took it and held it up really high, and everybody started to sing; and looking at that Plate up so high in the air, I was moved to sing mournfully right along with them.

After that I was a Dog of Diminished Expectations, so I curled up in a ball to get a little R & R in case the pack decided to make another run later.

They all sang some more, and the Nice Man named Ned and the Welcome Lady took turns talking. I believe they were trying to give the group some pointers on kicking up rabbits next time around.

Finally they gave a signal, and we all headed for the front of the church again. I braced for another hunt, but this time they all got down on their knees at the railing there and, lo and behold, here came the Welcome Lady around to each person in turn, and she, too, had a Plate! Smaller more my size- but a Plate all the same.

She came to my Person and gave her something to eat, and while she blessed Rita I put my nose through the rail and sniffed the plate, and looked as cute as I knew how… but there was to be no nosh for the dog this morning. Sad.

But then the Welcome Lady smiled so pretty and asked my Person, "Would Jack like to have a blessing?" And she put her hand on my head and said the very kindest words you could imagine. I forgot all about the plate, and my happy tail took over instead. ...

Once I was blessed we marched back to our seats, (no rabbit run this time), and sang some more, then everybody went back to the room where we came in to make our farewells.

I collected a whole bunch more of warm words and ear scratches, and the gentleman with the Big Plate said I had fine lines, and I was welcome back any time, that I sort of livened things up.

I am told he is a connoisseur of beagles, so I was honored and proud.

My person and I got back in our car and headed home, and curled up on the seat in the warm sunshine, I knew I had in fact been blessed.

And I had a little time to think about the Nice Man Ned and the Welcome Lady, and I decided they had taught the pack a pretty good lesson that morning:

If you all run around and sing as loud and pretty as you can with all your heart and still can't kick up a rabbit in ten passes, you need to head home for chow and a long nap, and save the hunt for another day.

I hope to go back again sometime. I felt a bond with all those good folks, and I'm looking forward to seeing that nice pack again. Maybe they'll let me take the lead on the next hunt. I could really help with their singing, and with my expertise, I'll guarantee if there's a rabbit in that Church, I'll flush him out!

Probably not *next* Sunday, though... Easter's not a good Sunday for rabbit-hunting.

Chapter Forty-One

A Fable about Big Jugs

When Jack Beagle was measured in months rather than years I was at wit's end trying to find something more constructive to amuse him than chewing on computer cables and game controllers.

A couple of kind friends had given me the equivalent of "Beagles for Beginners" books, and both books mentioned the affinity beagles have for puzzles, or "figgerin' stuff out".

They mentioned the hard rubber toys that are made for hiding treats as being a nice challenge.

I didn't have one of those, but ordered one, and while I was waiting for it, took an empty half-gallon plastic milk jug and put an assortment of small treats in it and put it on the foot stool to see what might happen.

Jack thought it was the finest thing since canned viennas...

It made a WONDERFUL RACKET as it bounced and rattled, every now and then releasing a treat.

He quickly became so proficient that he had a dent in the other end of the jug to bite to make it easy to flip the contents out more efficiently.

It wasn't long before he would bring the jug for a refill as many times a day as I could be had... (This is not to be mistaken for "fetching". Beagles neither fetch nor catch, seeing such pursuits as a total waste of time, saying with that LOOK "...and why would I do that??" A beagle lives a purpose driven life.)

That game went on all winter, I'm happy to say.

Spring came and I was sitting on the deck, Jack in the yard, when we noticed at about the same moment that a neighbor's dog had dragged into our yard a WHOLE GALLON-SIZED empty milk jug, and left it.

Honest to Pete, I could see Jack's brain smoking: "If I get x amount of treats in the jug I have now, just think what I can get with this one!"

He ran out and picked up the jug, got up a good head of steam, and came **flying** to bring it up on the deck, head full of sugarplums yet to come.

Unfortunately, he forgot to calculate the increased girth of the new jug, and how that might affect his ascent of the stairs. He tore to the deck, wide open, hit the steps and BOOSH, head over teakettle he went.

Jack doesn't normally swear a lot, but he was a little dazed and he shook his head as if to say "What the @&#$ just happened??"

After I picked myself up off the deck where I'd collapsed laughing (of course not AT Jack... hahahahahah), I retrieved his trophy and took it in the house wherein it became the new standard for what constitutes a fair serving of treats.

In subsequent seasons Jack found that human beings are reasonably easy to train, especially the ones that understand beagle-speak. Aunt Skits was the first trained to load the jug with treats, followed by Cousin Clay, Roger, and Carson, who can all take the hint at the first rattle of the magic container.

Jack never saw training our friend Tank as a good move, because Tank, on Sundays, stops at the store and brings Jack a whole bacon-egg-cheese biscuit. I think Jack saw the possibility that in learning to fill the Jug, Tank might forget the biscuit.

(Confession time: When Tank comes in with that wonderful still warm biscuit for Jack, I get a tinge of that "what-am-I-chopped-liver?" feeling; and seeing lust in my eyes, Tank has offered to bring me one too, but I know I really don't need a Sunday Biscuit, though one Sunday I just couldn't resist, and Jack's biscuit was two bites smaller.)

So... back to the Big Jug:

Last night I had settled down to watch the news, Jack Beagle and Lexie-da-Cat being settled in the kitchen, I assumed, in their usual you-be-nice-to-me, I'll-be-nice-to-you mode, when suddenly all hell broke loose.

I yelled "KNOCK THAT OFF!" and stood up to go break it up when this Monster went clattering by, knocking over everything in its path. It was part Black Cat and part Big Jug as it tore thru the living room plowing a path of destruction.

Finally, the Jug turned loose of the Cat, who disappeared into wherever cats go when cat-astrophe occurs, turning up unharmed much later, sporting that accusing look cats always have when they have been less than bright: "I know you did that to me, I just don't know how"…

I've since tried to reconstruct events. Jack's no help at all, since he's still rolling on the floor laughing (ROFL in beagle-speak).

I have to conclude that after five years of watching that foolish beagle behavior, Curiosity finally got the better of ol' Lex and she put her paw in the Jug to see what was so great about it, and it didn't come right out when she made a move to withdraw… and…*panic*!

The moral of this Fable:

> ***Big Jugs: Handle with care or they'll attack and knock you on your keister.***

Chapter Forty-Two

The Moonlight Run of Jack Beagle

Or

How I Spent the Night on the Sofa and the Day in the Doghouse

Jack Beagle left early in the morning for a run with his lady friend, Hershey.

His stomach generally brings him home shortly after dark, when the rabbits have retired for the evening, but on this particular night the moon was full and the rabbits in a party mood, so when I went to get Jack, he wagged his tail furiously and beagle-barked "Woman, can't you see I'm busy here??" and then ignored me completely.

Jack wears a tracker, a tiny little gizmo with about a day's battery life, so I can, unless he's in a dead zone for signals, see him on my computer and/or phone. Happily the signal was good and I knew where he was as the night went on: he was chasing the same dumb-bunny around in the same circle hour after hour…

At 10 p.m. I went out to try to lure him in with treats. His girl said "Thanks", ate three biscuits, and kept on going. Jack never took his nose off the ground.

Given my "druthers" I prefer to have the Beagle on site before I go to bed upstairs, since I'm not really wild about schlepping all the way downstairs at 3 a.m. to let the Prodigal in; so when 12 o'clock came and Jimmy Fallon was getting ready to hang it up I decided the easiest solution was, as I have done before, to stretch out on the sofa downstairs.

I knew he wouldn't be long, because I could see on the tracker Jack was headed home, about ten minutes out, normally; but there must have been many, many wonderful scents on the wind, because I was halfway asleep by 12:45 when the door sensor finally went off and Joe Cool showed up.

I proceeded to give Joe Cool a pretty good piece of my mind about keeping me up all night when I had to be up by 6:30 next morning. I was on a roll with the "YOUNG MAN WHAT DO YOU THINK YOU ARE DOING KEEPING ME UP ALL HOURS OF THE NIGHT…" yadda da yadda da yadda…

And then Jack did what he always does when I get mad with him— Gave me a dog-shoulder-shrug, rolled his eyes, as if to say "I don't need this grief!" turned his back on me and trudged upstairs to bed!

I decided that since the night was half over I might as well finish it out on the sofa, so I curled up and went to sleep at last.

Sometime around 3 or 4 a.m. I woke and hung my hand down off the sofa and felt beagle. I gave him a pat on the back to let him know I still loved him.

He didn't respond at all, just so I wouldn't think he'd forgiven me for being so brazen as to give him a hard time; and his body English was most eloquent: "Don't make a big deal of it that I'm sleeping on the floor beside you. It doesn't mean a thing. It's not that I care at all if the lions and bears and coyotes eat you, I'm just more comfortable sleeping on this hard floor beside you than in my stressless chair upstairs!"

In the morning I was ready to kiss and make up but the big chill was still in effect, and it wasn't until evening that I'd finally coughed up enough treats, belly-rubs and rump-scratches to get a feeble tail wag, indicating I might someday be forgiven for my transgressions.

The thing that escapes me in all of this is: given the events of the evening, how come I'm the one who wound up in the Dog House?!?

Chapter Forty-Three

Ramblin' Man

J. Beagle has established a fine rapport with his neighbors, and lest you think I have somewhat exaggerated his skills in communication, I offer these testimonials from friends J.B. visits regularly on his rounds:

Neighbor Jeff said "Jack and I were sitting on the steps out back, looking at the pigs, and I said 'Jack, you've probably never seen a pig before...'. He looked like he was real interested in them, and we sat there for a long time studying them before he decided to move on..."

Neighbor Vernon and I were taking a break from spraying the Christmas trees and Vernon said "Jack stopped by yesterday while I was working on the tractor and stayed to visit a while. I said to him, 'Jack, I hear you running all over the place, sounding like a serious hunting dog... but I'll bet you haven't ever caught one of those rabbits!'... and you know, he turned around and gave me a drop-dead-buddy look and left!"

Had a phone call from Neighbor Leslie, a mile or so down the road, one afternoon. She said "I just wanted to let you know Jack's over here at my place. He's lying on the sofa on my porch... I think he's waiting for you to give him a ride home."

One pleasant evening I was out looking for Jack and neighbor David Carroll flagged me down... he just wanted to let me know Jack had been there most of the day trying to teach his dog Jake, a Golden, to be a rabbit dog.

When Roger comes to mow the trees I always have Vienna sausages for him. I'll say "I put out two cans, but Jack doesn't need but two or three sausages." When I come home later, Roger says "Jack said three of those little viennies wouldn't do it, so he had one can and I had the other one."

Tank comes in on Sunday mornings, and Jack's tail starts going as soon as the driveway alert sounds. Sure enough, most Sundays Tank has stopped at the Glenmore Grocery and picked up a sausage and scrambled egg biscuit for Jack. Thank goodness, he hands it to me so I can ration it out, minus most of the bread, over the day.

One day Tank came in for lunch and said "Jack's mad at Skitsy." I said "How could you tell?" Tank: "He went and barked at her door for a treat and she didn't come, so he barked louder. She still didn't come, so he barked even louder... then when she still didn't come he got mad and left!"

So... it wasn't surprising when last week Neighbor John called (he lives next door to Leslie). He said Jack had run right up to him, not what he usually does... he usually keeps his distance so no one can catch him and put a damper on his fun; but this time he was limping badly on one leg. I'm guessing that Jack figured that if Leslie had a way to communicate with me that Jack needed a ride home, John would be able to do that too...

Chapter Forty-Four

Jack Beagle Invents a New Game

First thing in the morning, when I have my nose stuck in a puzzle book as I try persuade my brain to come to the party, I hear Jack doing his morning dance, a rowdy rumba which entails noisily scratching his rump on the undersides of both of the stressless footstools upstairs… Makes a great clatter and a bang, and leaves the footstools nowhere near the chairs they were meant for.

Then things go silent as the new game begins…

I look up from my book and see what appears to be a disembodied pair of eyes and ears peering down at me in a decidedly crocodilian manner from under the bottom balcony rail.

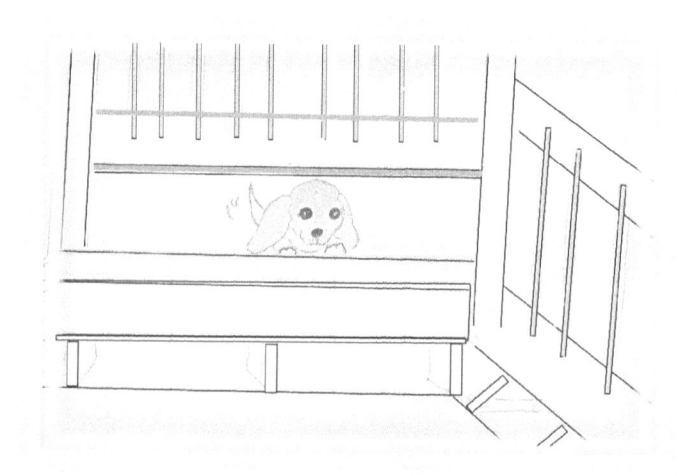

My play: "I think I heard a puppy…"
Jack: No sound or motion.
Me, hopefully, tentatively: "I think it might be MY puppy…
Jack, dead quiet, still playing crocodile, eyes sparkling…
Me… "Maybe it's… JACK!"
By now the invisible back end of the dog is wagging so hard that the ears on the front end are jiggling in the breeze, clearly indicating that I'm being pranked.

… and when we can't bear the suspense any longer, 29 pounds of happy beagle comes bounding down the stairs, laughing all the way because he played such a fine joke on me:

"SURPRISE! It's ME!

At this point my part in the game is to shout

"YES, it IS! It IS my Puppy!!"

He pauses for an ear scratch or a fast belly rub, "Good Morning", runs to the sofa, buries his head in his favorite velvet pillow, and goes back to sleep.

Game over …

New day properly initiated.

Chapter Forty-Five

Possum in the Road

So last night I was out looking for Jack Beagle and was passed by a large black SUV moving out smartly down the road.

I poked along behind at my leisurely dog-spotting pace and noticed in the dark a largish clump in the road that looked like it might possibly have breathed at one time (before the large SUV passed). It never budged, so I straddled it and proceeded down the road, and when unsuccessful in my quest to find Jack, I turned around and headed back home.

The pile of whatever-it-was was still in the road, so I straddled it yet again.

Got home and waited a while, hoping JB's tracker would turn up on the computer, but he was incommunicado.

I headed out again, slowed down at the lump in the road to be sure it wasn't Jack, defunct and covered in road dust. Nope, just a messy looking pile… Straddled it again and continued down the road.

This time Jack Beagle showed up at last, ready to go home for supper, so I turned around and headed back home…

… just in time to see the lump in the road stand and become Mr. Possum, rising like a phoenix from the ashes, just stretching his legs when he saw me coming.

He turned his head toward me and his whole body spoke volumes….

"C'mon...Really? ...You??...Again???"

I stopped cold and waited while he stomped indignantly across the road.

First time I've ever been chastised by a possum....

Chapter Forty-Six

Whistlin' Jack

So… In a move by yours truly to avoid driving 3,000 miles per year looking for him, Jack Beagle now wears a tracker.

The tiny communicator has saved me untold miles and untold agony, fearing he was in the wrong place, wrong time and I'd never see his dear Beagle Face at the door again.

The tracker is a fine contraption with the absolute coolest tech support in the world… Can you imagine dealing all day every day with hysterical people who are frantic about their pets? The tech support folks for the tracker are the ultimate in calming hysterical parents.

I know this because I've been on the receiving end of their infinitely patient TLC on several occasions. One especially notable time was when I hadn't fastened the tracker to the collar properly, which caused it to fall off in the middle of a heavy growth of cedars. Panic! Not only did I not know where Jack was, neither did I know where the tracker was.

Jack wandered in eventually to my great relief, and early, early next morning friend Rita and I set out to try to find the tracker, which was advising us plaintively from somewhere in the stratosphere that "Jack's battery needs charging".

In desperation I called Tech Support for help, and at the same time ordered another tracker, so sure was I that the lost one was gone forever.

The Tech advised me that since the tracker was in the safe zone, if I unplugged the charger, the satellite would be able to locate the tracker, so I did, and… dog if it didn't do just that! We were guided right to it in the deep woods.

I would not like to replicate that exercise, but it was surely impressive.

Soooo… anyhow… These days, armed with his tracker, Jack sets out on his daily rounds.

I am convinced from neighbors' remarks that he carries a list in his vest pocket (rather like Martha Stewart's monthly schedule), of the neighborhood activities that he tracks. It must read something like this:

"Monday… everybody working, no cookouts; Stop by for chat with Vernon… look out, school bus runs at 4:15; Wed: sometimes Mt. View neighbor throws good scraps out; Thurs: check western neighbor's yard to see if her dog's food dish is outside; Sat: check on new pups with neighbors at ancestral home; evening, stop by to visit new neighbor on hill; if he's home for the weekend, he'll cook a hot dog each for Hershey and me. He told my Mom he knew we'd eat them cold, but he thought we really enjoyed them more grilled. Another real Prince of a man".

And so it goes thru the week. I'm sure even his Palm Sunday visits to church are on his rather comprehensive list.

With this list in pocket, Jack sets out on his daily rounds like a preacher riding circuit, with his best bud, Hershey, a mostly Labrador dowager retriever plodding along beside him.

Theirs is a symbiotic relationship: they both enjoy having someone to pal around with; Jack enjoys Hersheys' being a much bigger buddy when the going gets tough, and Hershey keeps pretending she's a rabbit dog in the wild hope that sooner or later Jack's going to kick up something for her to retrieve. (Also, I do think Jack likes to delude himself that he is responsible for Hersh's recent two litters of puppies, despite his having been "tutored" as a very young fellow. I haven't the heart to tell him.)

When the days are of a reasonable length, it's still just dusky when I head out to pick Jack up. As I close in on his most recent location guided by the tracker, I tap the horn in the "shave and a haircut" tattoo, and sometimes he's ready to quit and comes to the car with Hersh for their treats.

Mostly he's NOT ready: "Baroo ! can't you see I'm busy here, woman? Baroooo"!

Then I wait… and wait…

On easy days, Hershey appears like a friendly shadow and whispers "For a couple of those treats, I'll rat Jack out for you…"

I'm not proud. Hersh gets her treats in a timely manner, crunching loudly and happily away… and sure enough, pretty soon Jack comes strolling out of the brush and over to the car. My feeling is that this is simply because, being a Beagle, J.B. can't bear to have someone else eating while he is not. When not Nose-Driven, he's a Stomach-Driven kind of guy.

At this point Jack hops in the car, and there are treats all 'round. When I offer Hershey a ride she says once again, "No thanks, I don't get in cars", and we all head home according to our wonts, sometimes with Jack sitting on my lap, his foot on the mirror control button, "driving" while he adjusts the passenger side mirror so it is always looking at Jupiter.

Since I'm seldom on the outside passenger side of my car to correct the mirror, and he's gone waaay past detent using the inside button, when I make my weekly town trip there is always the normal hustle bustle of traffic behind me in the left lane, and nothing but clear blue sky behind me on the right!

Now we are in Winter's doldrums though, and the shorter days mean it's pretty darn dark when it's time for Jack to come home. Now when I click the "update location" on my phone, Jack's tracker strobes brightly, lighting up as it answers my search signal; and since the new tracker he just acquired has a much better battery and a much clearer lens, there is no chance of his hiding his light under a bushel.

I have noticed since the darker days and the newer tracker, instead of my having a long wait, Jack is frequently waiting right beside the road as I drive up. This is a nice surprise, but has been a bit of a pleasant puzzle. I do think though that I'm beginning to get the picture (of course this is pure conjecture on my part…)

In my mind's eye I see Jack and Hersh indulging in their last hunting and tracking spasm of the day when suddenly out of nowhere, Jack's neck starts lighting up like a firefly on steroids. Hersh takes one long, sad-eyed look of exasperation and says "Okay, buddy, time to pack it in", and she starts plodding homeward.

Jack, who has the pesky light under his chin where it's not so bothersome, yells after her "Wait, wait, no need to quit so soon... Baroo... I'm not done yet... C'mon, Hersh, one more round..."

At this, Hershey casts her baleful retriever eyes over at Jack and says quietly to her hyper companion:

"C'mon, yourself... I hear the horn, your Mom's on her way.... Might's well go stand by the road and get our treats. It's one thing for you to be always runnin' and hollerin'... but no self-respecting rabbit would be found within six miles of this place with you lightin' up like a pool hall on a Saturday night!..."

As I said, one can only surmise... but it's the only scenario that seems to fit.

Thanks, Hersh. Keep bringing him home...

Chapter Forty-Seven

Episcomouse and the Antependium

or *The Mouse in the Organ*

antependium. *plural antependiums or antependia \-dē-ə\ :a hanging for the front of an altar, pulpit, or lectern)*

The antependium at Emmanuel Church was magnificent green brocade.

Few of his race had ever had free and complete access to such splendid building material, and so he worked, slowly and with great care, constructing a home worthy of himself and the peaceful venue.

He was seldom interrupted. Oh yes, every couple of weeks he'd hear stirring around outside, lots of "amens" and "alleluias"... and some singing of variable quality but, no doubt, heartfelt sincerity; but for the most part, the world left him in peace, working away at weaving his masterpiece.

To be sure, there was that one cataclysmic day last September when he heard the shuffling around of two-footed creatures; and just when he had decided it was only more amens and alleluias as usual, and had curled himself up for a Sunday siesta, he was blown sky high out of his nest when someone sat down at the organ where he was building his domicile and ALL HELL BROKE LOOSE! Earthquake, typhoon, hurricane... his beautiful construct jumped up and down with the music, and he, helpless to do anything but a mad dance as the vibrations lifted and dropped him.

Apocalypse now!

And then, as suddenly as it had begun, it was over. He wiped his sweaty brow, and wished he could reach the refrigerator where the wine was kept...

The next day things were back to normal and so he resumed work on his palace.

He did so hope that none of the two-footed creatures noticed that the green brocade of the Pentecostal altar hanging was looking more than a little frayed; after all, he was only taking two or three threads at a time. And also, he most fervently hoped that his construction of a basement recreation room, which had put him squarely across the transistors and diodes that controlled C# and D, hadn't created a dissonance too noticeable. The organ was so seldom played, you wouldn't think anyone would've noticed ...

But when the fall of the year arrived, and he should have been spending more and more time in his cozy, luxurious surroundings, his small perfect world was completely disrupted by the arrival of The Organist.

From that day on, every other Sunday, his little world turned into a nightmare of eardrum-blasting sound and St. Vitus dance tremors, and oh—when a hymn had to be played in the key of A, with all those dissonant C#s,— it was just, well, God awful.

The two-footed folks apparently felt this too, and one Sunday after he had survived the bi-weekly musical trial by fire he settled in to enjoy a couple of weeks respite, and suddenly he heard a scratching and scraping outside the organ and the top was lifted off his world! A huge curious face peered in and he took off at a frantic pace for the cellar, and raced for the back door out...

He watched from a distance... (his kind and the bipedal folks never seemed to gee and haw)... and he was most gratified when they all gathered around to oooh and aaah over his opus magnum.

—and then they picked up his beautiful green brocade home and threw it in the trash!

He couldn't believe his eyes, but the truth was there before him…

He was as low as a little Episcomouse could be. All his love and labour, gone in one fell swoop.

He moped around day after day, so depressed he could hardly bring himself to get up in the morning, but with great effort, he managed to drag through each day; and one sunny morning as he yawned and stretched at the mousehole in the church foundation, he saw a sign across the road that said "Glenmore Methodist Church".

He scratched his head and studied that sign, and pondered the course of recent events, and he decided that it was in fact more than a sign, it was a portent; and it came to him that there was a lesson to be found in all this, to wit:

If the folks you're with don't treasure your treasures, it's time to find some folks who do!

So he packed his small valise and trudged across the road, his optimistic little soul recovering with every step.

Maybe he'd find RED brocade this time, and build again, bigger and better than ever!

Chapter Forty-Eight

Why I Love Buckingham...

Big storm passed through taking down some trees and limbs, and apparently, a few fences.

I went out to track Jack Beagle down and head him toward home, and found myself behind a Friday afternoon cow—you know, the one made just before quitting time. I followed it along for half a mile or so and finally got a good side view, and lo and behold, realized it was a zebu!

Took me a minute or two to absorb this big wrinkle in my daily routine, but once I had determined that I was not hallucinating, I decided that any self-respecting zebu owner would want to be informed.

From my car I phoned a neighbor who, in a whole raft of unflappable neighbors, is probably at the top of the heap: "I'm down on Logan Road following behind what appears to be a zebu?!"

I expected a little amazement. I myself had never seen a zebu in person before, but no... With casual nonchalance my good neighbor says "Yep... she belongs to one of the neighbors over this way. I'll give him a call..."

The zebu, meantime, had moseyed over to the car window as if to listen in on the conversation, and when I rang off, switched her tail and nodded as if to say "Thanks, been trying to get back through that blame fence for an hour." —then she turned and ambled off.

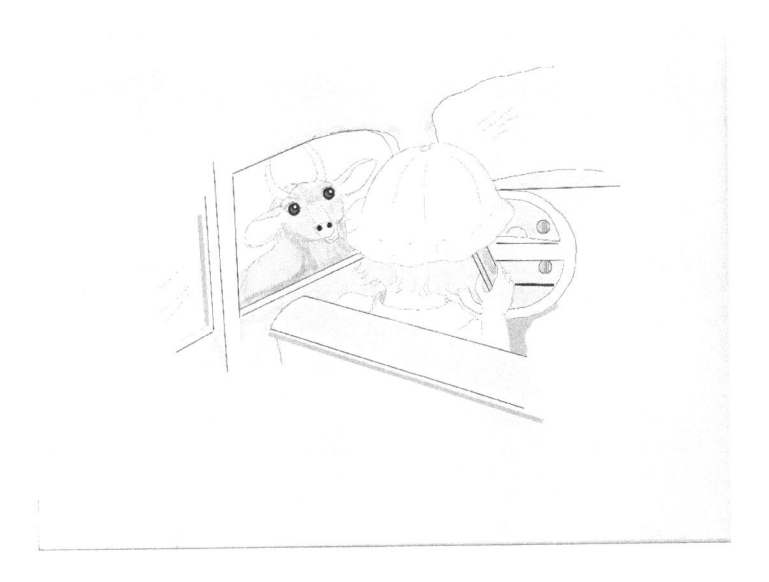

When I came back through that stretch she was no longer there. I assume she was safely back home with her flock of little zebus and her knitting.

Score one for an interesting day at the zoo....

Later

Over the years in earliest spring at dusk I've had to stop in the road for a very smitten ruffed grouse, so in love my car went unnoticed.

A few mornings ago there was a largish bird sitting low on Neighbor Bob's fence, so surprising that I had to stop and let my brain start indexing: hawk, nope, owl, nope, pigeon, nope... then the bird straightened up to show off head-shape and tail, and sure enough, it was a grouse!.

This one is apparently either unsmitten as yet, or sooo over it. What a treat to see, and also to know they're a growing population, as this one is 3-4 miles from my old faithful.

So now for March, that's one zebu; two or three rainbows, depending on how you count double rainbows; and a grouse!

Spring—I'm loving it!

About the Author

Elizabeth "Betsy" Samuels grew up in Virginia Beach when it was a mere hamlet in winter and a family resort in summer.

An avid reader even as a youngster, Betsy became acquainted early on with the gentle irreverence of James Thurber, Mark Twain, Erma Bombeck, and Betty MacDonald. It is her hope that her own writing brings the same "laugh at our foibles and love us anyway" sort of wit and wisdom that those wonderful authors have brought to the Buffet Table of Life.

Betsy now owns and operates Foxfire Christmas Tree Farm in Buckingham County, Virginia, where she continues collecting tales of the Off-the-Wall and the Downright Peculiar.